Alexander Ewing

# An address to the younger clergy and laity on the present state of religion

Being some contribution towards a defence of the Church of England

Alexander Ewing

**An address to the younger clergy and laity on the present state of religion**
*Being some contribution towards a defence of the Church of England*

ISBN/EAN: 9783337184896

Printed in Europe, USA, Canada, Australia, Japan

Cover: Foto ©Lupo / pixelio.de

More available books at **www.hansebooks.com**

# An Address

## TO THE

# YOUNGER CLERGY AND LAITY

### ON THE

## PRESENT STATE OF RELIGION,

#### BEING SOME CONTRIBUTION TOWARDS

## A DEFENCE OF THE CHURCH OF ENGLAND.

### BY

## THE BISHOP OF ARGYLL.

'The Word of God is not bound.'—2 Tim. ii. 9.

LONDON:
LONGMAN, GREEN, LONGMAN, ROBERTS, & GREEN.
1865.

# ADDRESS.

\* \* \* \* Let us now turn from our special affairs to those general questions which affect the Church at large. And first to those which have created so much discussion of late—the questions brought for decision before the highest Tribunal in the Church of England, the Privy Council, and which have been of such general interest to all intelligent members of our Communion. It will be in your memories that when I last addressed you in Diocesan Synod, I made allusion to these questions. They were then at issue and awaiting decision.

Since that decision, I have addressed you in a pastoral letter, a copy of which every instituted incumbent of this diocese, I trust, has received. This makes it less necessary that I should say much to you on the subject at this present moment. I shall therefore add but a few words to what I have previously said; a few words of caution and of encouragement to which my office binds me. May the Holy Spirit of truth and charity bless and guide me in this as in all things.

No doubt it may be held (as it was in the previous case of the Gorham judgment) that we are not so affected by the decisions of the Church of England as to be bound by them, but considering that we have adopted the standards and formularies of the Church of England, I do not think that there can be any moral question that we are bound to accept these Standards in the sense that the Church, from which we take them, receives them. If a legal question should arise involving the point, it is most probable that it would be decided on this aspect.

From time to time, no doubt, a difficulty may arise as to the sense in which the Church of England holds them. At present this question is decided by the Supreme Court of Ecclesiastical Judicature in England, the Privy Council.

The Privy Council consists of the two Archbishops and of the Metropolitan Bishop of the Church of England, of the Queen and of certain Christian Laity nominated by the Crown, and generally taken from the highest ranks of the legal profession.

The powers of the court are limited: it gives no utterance to new dogma, it but interprets the meaning of the old.

It brings to this investigation both those professionally interested in the subjects under decision, and those who are not so, and also minds familiar with questions of interpretation, and of documentary evidence.

The Queen, as head over all, secures that protection be equally afforded to all her subjects under the jurisdiction of this tribunal.

This is the mode whereby is decided the meaning of the Standards of the Church of England. It is difficult to conceive any method which could be adopted more efficacious.

The Church of England is not in a position to draw out new articles of faith. She can merely give her interpretation of the old. And this can alone be done by ascertaining the legitimate meaning of her Standards, or by preventing the adoption of that which is contrary to it. For such purpose all that is requisite is a court of sufficient capacity and integrity as may be able and willing to give such interpretation.

Such a Court undoubtedly is provided in the Judicial Committee of the Privy Council. The questions lately brought before it were, the force of the terms 'Eternal punishment,' the extent and nature of the 'Inspiration of Holy Scripture,' the sense of the word 'Substitution,' in the Atonement; and (previously in the Gorham case) that of 'Regeneration' in Baptism.

On these subjects the Court was called upon to decide, and to give the sense of the Church of England. The decision of the Court was, that in none of the cases had the doctrine complained of (as being taught by specified clergymen) exceeded a fair interpretation of the Standards.

The Court did not lay down new definitions.

It will generally be considered that the Court in doing so acted wisely. It had no power to decide such questions by new definitions of faith. It would have been inexpedient to have claimed such power. The questions were questions which had never been previously decided by the Church at large, and not having been decided by the Church as a whole, it was not in the power of the Church of England to decide them as a part.

And there are some questions which the Church at large cannot decide. She can make no addition to the knowledge of the Divine nature. She cannot add to Holy Scripture. She cannot add any new fact to Revelation. At the best, she is the interpreter, the witness, and keeper, the pillar and ground of Holy Writ. She is not the origin of Revelation.

Revelation comes, not from the Church, but to the Church. Revelation comes to the Church, and she makes it known. She is called to be a faithful and true witness, but nothing more. If this is all that she can be when considered as a whole, she cannot be more than this when existing but as a part. Definitions of the faith delivered by the Church as a whole, would be valuable were they to be obtained; they cannot be obtained, and in such-a-case the definitions by a part are of limited value. The churches of Jerusalem, Alexandria, Antioch, and of Rome (we say) have erred. We cannot claim exemption for the Church of England or lay down her decisions as infallible. This being so, any decision of matters of faith on her own account would have been inexpedient. Particular Churches may enact bye-laws for their own particular guidance. They cannot with propriety legislate on matters common to the Church at large. Holy Scripture containeth all things necessary for salvation. As the Church at large has never laid down any authoritative interpretation of it, it cannot be incumbent on any portion to do so. We cannot suppose such to be necessary, or it would have been done. The Holy Spirit is promised to us individually to lead us into all truth; beyond this there is no promise and no security.

But additions to Holy Scripture have even failed on those points which it might have been thought they would secure, the unity and uniformity of the faithful. The additions made to the Apostle's Creed by the Nicene Council went far to cause the division of the Eastern and Western Churches. The Creed of Athanasius now severs some of the Western from the Eastern Churches, the additions of Trent have tended to circumscribe Latin Christianity, and the confessions of Augsburg, Geneva, France, Scotland, and America, have done more to sever each from the other, and from the Church at large, than to add to the meaning of Revelation.

Knowing this and more than this, the Church of England abstained with a becoming reticence from laying down any new definition or giving any dogmatic utterance. On the points lately submitted to her, she ruled that Holy Scripture (as her Standards rule) containeth all things necessary for salvation, and she gave no new interpretations of her Standards. The main aspect of her utterance was negative, she did not so much decide as decline to decide, nor define as refuse to define, on the subjects brought before her. She knew that new decisions on the faith were beyond her power, and that the old required no addition. She maintained the integrity of her Standards, and the sufficiency of Holy Scripture; beyond this she did not go, and we think that the wisdom of her decision will be more apparent as years roll on to show it. One and a constantly recurring difficulty in such religious decisions must and ever will be, to what extent (if any) the civil government of a country should be concerned in such determinations. Whether and to what extent the Crown should have part in the councils of Religion? A question which will be determined differently in all probability, as he who judges inclines either to the view of the unity of end of all external government, or to that of its diversity.

Looking at Christianity as the highest good for man, and essentially the same in the ruler and the ruled, it is more easy to see why the Crown should have part in all councils held for its advancement than why it should not. And it argues a defective view of Christianity, and gives it a lower position than its due, when it can be separated from other means for the well-being of a community. The Crown and the Crozier are but different instruments towards one end, and both equally servants of it. If these two can be combined in one, it would seem the highest form to which they can attain, and the best for a country. To separate David the King from Zadok the Priest, is an evil office for Israel. And no doubt it is only when righteousness is (in idea) divided, and made into instrumental and external, as different from real and actual, that this is done. Then different office bearers are appointed, and the officers are separate. We have seen the combinations of both forms in the Papacy and in its Pagan predecessor in Rome, in both of which the civil and religious idea was combined under one head, in the first the religious, in the second the secular element preponderating. In both cases they broke down, from the infirmity of human nature diverting their existence for the general good, to personal ends.

At present, in England, the work is divided, and the officers of both departments perform their labour together. It is a lowering of the ideal to the actual, but in our present state it is the utmost which can be attempted. It is a mutual compact; as it were that of husband and wife, accompanied with some articles of definition and agreement, but based upon mutual confidence and devotion to a common object, the well-being of the country, and as the ultimate result of this, the perfection of its Christianity. The secular, which is the rougher element, and the religious, that which elevates and subdues this, acting on one another for their own mutual benefit.

If at any time the softer influence seems to lose its hold—as it is its bounden duty and object to civilise and elevate the other, its business is to endeavour to regain its ground. She has but a feeble idea of a wife who, on any hardness, thinks it best for her to forsake her husband. But when this influence is extreme, it requires a moderator. From the very magnitude of the interests at stake, the priesthood is apt to disregard all considerations other than the accomplishment of their special object. It is well for them when the coarser element is able and willing to moderate their aims in this behalf. It is clear that, in the highest example of all, the Roman Governor, had he acted up to what he felt to be his duty, should have controlled the violence of the priesthood—that Gallio did well for the Church and himself, in saving the life of Paul—that the civil power did badly for itself and for the Church when yielding to the influence of an excited religion in Piedmont, in France, in Holland, in Scotland and elsewhere, the civil arm was made the instrument of religious executions. It is better for religion to feel the force of the secular arm herself (as in Apostolic and other times), than that the world should feel oppression at the instance of religion. Happily, at this moment, by a wise arrangement, both forces are united in one combination in England, and so long as the Articles of Agreement are maintained, and the object for which they themselves exist are kept in view, the Ministers of State and of Religion will preserve their union. On a late occasion, in the decisions of the Privy Council now under consideration, care was taken that these articles should not be infringed.

These observations on the general policy of the Church are all which I shall venture to offer at this time. The principles which underlie them are very important, but too extensive to be properly treated of here, even were I capable of doing justice to them. They are, however, so necessary to be clearly understood, that a few words towards a right apprehension of them may not be unacceptable.

The principles which are involved in the religious questions of the day are mainly these: The basis on which Revelation rests; the mode in which it accomplishes its objects; and the relation which authority bears towards it.

The basis on which Revelation rests, of course, is its own truth, received primarily through the spiritual discernment, the understanding and the conscience, with which we are endowed, and to which it is addressed.

Our blessed Lord infers this, when He asks, 'Why of your own selves judge ye not that which is right?' and St. Paul, when he says, that 'the law is written on men's hearts;' and where he urges them to understand 'what the will of the Lord is;' and again where he commends his teaching to men's consciences. All the Law and the Gospel, and all Divine communication of whatever nature, come to man on this supposition.

The mode in which Revelation accomplishes its object we shall understand most easily, if we bear in mind what that object is. It is to bring men nigh to God. To bring them nigh, not in the sense of external relation, but of unity of nature. The human is to be made divine; the son of Adam to become a son of God; and a son not with the obedience of a servant, but with the liberty of a child. 'God hath spoken unto us by His Son,' 'that,' says St. John, 'we may have fellowship with the Father.' Such being the object, let us see how it is to be accomplished.

Man is to be partaker of the Divine nature. For this purpose much is required. Man must be good with moral goodness. Good, in the moral sense, that is, by *choosing* to be good; there can be no other moral goodness. To accomplish this, special conditions are required; conditions which involve time and circumstances. Man must have power to choose, and a variety to choose from; he must obtain knowledge, and that from experience.

Such a creation cannot be the product of 'fiat,' or of a single operation; it must be the product of time and of progress.

Created for this end, God bestows on man capacities to secure it. Designed in the image of God, in the likeness of His Christ (who is the Head of man, the Divine ideal for every man), in and by Christ (the life of Christ becoming the life of every man), the end is to be arrived at.

It is plain that the end is only to be attained by measure and in degree. When far advanced on the way, an Apostle says, 'he had not yet attained' it. It is a process and a progress; an 'increase in wisdom and stature,' in knowledge and conformity to the will of God,—an increase and progress, as we use the means and faculties which God bestows upon us for this purpose.

It is a divine life and a new birth, and as such cannot be ours but with pain and difficulty, with groaning and travailling. The creature is subjected to vanity; put under conditions of darkness and bondage, that he may attain this regeneration, and by attaining it acquire the glorious liberty of a son of God. It is an high end—it cannot be attained but by corresponding means. It is far off, and complicated; <u>it can only be had as the product of a work,</u> by a process of choosing and refusing; of sowing and reaping; of tasting and proving the nature of things, and holding fast that which is good. It is a process not dissimilar to the bodily process—as the bodily life and health are sustained and increased by food and labour, so is the spiritual by knowledge, by antagonism, by spiritual exercise, by increase in the knowledge of God, by going on to perfection,—a perfection through suffering, by laying down the animal nature. This life is acquired by seeking and searching, by discerning and holding fast that which is good. Its end is the result of a process, not the product of a law; it is the attainment of a nature which no regulative code could give. It is a life got by education—an education evolving a higher life. If we see this we shall understand why it is that we are circumstanced as we are, why it is that we are surrounded with our present environments, dark Providences, God's word in earthen vessels, divisions in His Church. Nothing is made certain to us until we make it so to ourselves through search and through experience, that we may not slumber, or mistake the sign for the substance. There is infallible guidance, but it is in the shepherding of God, not in the words of a formula.

The way is needful for the end; the end is high, the way uphill. The end is peace, but it is only possible through victory. Jacob wrestling with the angel is the Scriptural type of it. A struggle with the unknown, and in the dark; a wrestling with something which makes the creature to halt on its thigh, but ends by leaving him transfigured into a Prince with God. This is the end, and how it is to be accomplished The way and the end. Revelation is the means.

Do *we* shrink from the way? No doubt we do. The spirit may be willing, but the flesh is weak. Many, yea, most, desire another way, a shorter way, or some substitute for the way; and many substitutions have been attempted, but they cannot, and do not, give the end; they only give that which they contain, and that is a very different end—at the best but leanness and barrenness to the soul.

The Roman and Eastern Churches (and too many Protestants also) substitute authority and privilege for the way; and the result is, the unreal and powerless Christianity we behold. The guide is substituted for the thing he guides to; the door for the interior; the name for the kingdom.

Revelation gives a new nature, a new world, a new kingdom, a possession which, if we know it not, we have it not. It is a condition which can have no substitute; if we feel it not, we have it not. It is righteousness, peace, and joy in the Holy Ghost, and all that we can know of the Holy Ghost is that which we experience of the Holy Ghost. We have it not, if we know it not.

Sometimes we put away the end, as well as the way; and this by a false humility. Let us observe this. We are called by God to the fellowship of love; and we say, 'Depart from me, for I am a sinful man, O Lord.' The Lord descends to cleanse us, and we say 'Thou shalt never wash my feet.' Most natural and real are such sayings; but they are not the right sayings. True humility is to hear and to obey the Divine voice; and if the Lord bids us to open our mouths, to open them in full assurance that He knows best what He means.

There is a pseudo-meekness, a counterfeit humility, which putting the love of God from us with a false modesty, desires to be a servant, and not a son; a humility which would substitute obedience for sympathy; and distance from, for nearness to the Divine. Let us beware of this—let us understand the 'taking of the manhood into God.' It was a greater thing to lower the Deity to humanity, than to lift up the humanity to God. It is a prouder thing to refuse to hear, than to bend our ears. If we say 'such knowledge is above us'—it ought not so to be. If we know not these things, Revelation was given to teach them. If we are in darkness and the darkness comprehends them not, this should not be the case; the darkness ought to comprehend them. If we are baptised into the Divine Spirit, it is that we might have Divine light.

But let us return. The object of Revelation being the communication of a Divine life, and that life to be attained by the pursuance of a path which is productive of it, we have seen that, as we proceed on that path, we become aware of the reality and origin of that which is revealed, and this with an assurance which cannot be overthrown. We become not only assured of the correctness of the way, from its conducting to the end, but we are assured that the end is actual and is Divine, and this with a certainty based upon a different foundation from that which consists in acquiring a belief, or forming an opinion: it is a certainty arising out of the acquisition of a life, a new life; new, different, and higher in kind than the old, of the reality of which we are assured as we were of that of the old itself. When we have attained a measure of this life through the access which Revelation has had to us, the reality and Divine source of Revelation are placed on another basis—accomplishing the object for which it was sent, its own truth becomes manifest, and as before we reasoned forward from its fitness, so now we reason backward from its effects. The authenticity of Revelation, when placed on this basis, is unassailable, inasmuch as it is a basis which cannot be touched by the accidents, while it is free from the abuses and difficulties inseparable from other evidences. True it is, that it can be possessed but by a limited number; by those only who have undergone the process by which it is obtained; and that it cannot be demonstrated to those who have not obtained it; they cannot be made aware of it by the demonstration of which external evidence is capable; but its value is not the less for this. The Positivist may deny it, because it cannot be made manifest to him; as the untaught man may deny the possibility of conveying intelligence by letters. Let him go through the process of learning, however, and he will believe. Let the Positivist 'put on Christ,' —go through the process by which the Divine life is conveyed, and he will then confess the origin and the reality of Revelation.

It is possible that to this simple but all-powerful evidence we may be mainly reduced, to the power more than the word of Revelation, when the accidents which are the accidents inseparable from the preservation of external evidence, the discrepancy in the summaries of religious belief, the tendency to substitute the way for the end and other things, both for the way and the end (different forms of which errors at different times and places have reduced Christendom to that state in which we see it), render it needful for us that thus it should be. And it is not improbable that in the Divine counsels we are to be brought back to this authentication of Revelation, by being brought back to the actuality of Christianity by the possession, mainly that is, of its powers—a consummation from which indeed no pious mind will shrink.

Revelation acting on the basis of fitness and of the experience of its fulfilling its end is no doubt that which is most available to all ages and conditions, and that which is most easily brought to bear upon mankind. Other and valuable proofs there are, such as from tradition and authority, but the difficulties connected with them are great, and the present unsatisfactory state of Christendom is mainly owing to the abuse of them.

There is an instinct pervading Christendom that Christianity is assuredly true, and would be all that is required, if we had it as it was, and as it now exists in the Divine mind. Thoughtful men are disquieted by the fact of the existence of so many and so various definitions of it. They would have it, they say, as it came from God; as it has been in its essence everywhere and always, when held by true Christian men. It is the conclusion I believe, and the problem of the present Christian world. I do not believe that properly, it can be answered, but by the life of Christ becoming our life. I do not believe that there is any other sufficient answer. The faith of Christ, 'the faith once for all delivered to the saints,' is faith in what Christ was, as set forth in the Holy Scripture. He who sets forth this and commends it by, and experiences it in, his own life, does most towards the demonstration and the truth of Christianity. Christianity mainly based on external evidence, so hangs together that an injury to one part, is the destruction of the whole, an evidence not only imperfect, but improper to depend on, for it cannot be (for example) true, that if some of the Old Testament (let it be said) is human, Christianity is not Divine. Christianity is so Divine that it depends not on external or outer testimony. Although the result of Revelation, it is its own warrant, and it authorises Revelation, more than Revelation authorises it. External authority indeed (save in the sense of introducing and instructing) has no place in its authentication. Let us enquire, however, as fully as we can into the relation which authority bears to it. Authority can only bear an external and limited relation to Christianity. It is no portion of it, for it can be separated from it. No authority indeed is part of that which it exists to indicate. And this is especially true of authority having reference to spiritual things. It is possible to receive authority apart from any experience of the things which it comes to convey: it is possible to substitute it for these things: where this last is done, it proceeds necessarily to communicate something else in place of truth. In matters of revelation, when this takes place, authority is described as a taking away the key of knowledge or as anti-Christ sitting on the throne of God, or the sin which is unpardonable (as irremediable)—viz. confounding the eternal distinctions of good and evil, and arrogating to authority the power to make that to be which is not, according to its own word, and this we have seen done, until duty has been divorced from conscience, and the merit of faith made dependant on the distance it kept from reason.

We observe that authority which addresses our spiritual faculties is itself subject to them, for it derives its recognition from them. As these are the avenues by which spiritual communications reach us, so are they the bar at which they are judged. Whether man exercises his spiritual faculties on every occasion, as each object presents itself, or whether he abdicates their exercise by one act of judgment, it is the same thing; his spiritual faculties are the Court wherein he passes spiritual judgment; every man for himself. It must be so, there is no other tribunal; and in this matter no man can act for another. He may indeed depute another or defer his judgment to another's, but it is the same thing; it is his own act which rules him, his own judgment which decides. There is no escape from this, save by inaction, or being to spiritual things as if they were not. He who denies this power and freedom to man, denies his power of receiving spiritual instruction, and of the liberty to choose and to refuse, inherent in that image in which he was created. This is that right of private judgment (which is indeed a necessity) obscured in the middle ages, but cleared at the Reformation. Strange is it to hear members of a church partaking in that regeneration speak of it as the root of scepticism and unbelief. Without our possession of it, Revelation would have been addressed to us in vain. Because of its possession, and of all possessing it, it is addressed to us and to all; by awakening it, and our other spiritual faculties, and by their education and development it is, that Revelation effects its object for us; the bestowal on man of a Divine and Eternal Life.

Let us now consider of what Revelation consists, and how it is we attain its meaning, or what relation Revelation bears to what is called the Church.

Revelation we have concluded to be contained in Holy Scripture. There may be outside of the Bible portions of knowledge which may justly be called Revelation; but as Holy Scripture (as the Article well expresses it) 'contains all things necessary for salvation,' there is no need to travel beyond it in our definition. It may be also, that if not needful, those other things may be also untrue; they have no such warrant as that which Scripture has, and if doubtful and unnecessary had better be treated as such.

It is not alleged that all in Holy Scripture is necessary for salvation. Abraham, Moses, the Prophets, some of the Apostles themselves, the different Churches which received but their special epistle, were all without that fulness of communication which we reckon as, and include in, Holy Scripture. They had, however, sufficient. What may be sufficient of Holy Scripture or Revelation for an individual or a church, it is not needful to define, but when we think of the conversions made by the sermons of the first Apostles, and the summaries given by them, it is plain that the elements of salvation lie in a lesser compass than is generally supposed; and that, if these are present, we need not be over careful about things beyond. What these essentials are has been variously defined. They have been differently defined by different churches, and as interpretations of Holy Scripture these definitions have their value, but as definitions of the essentials of salvation they must not be considered as infallible. It is not the province of the Church (or Churches) to add to Holy Scripture, or to give to interpretations the same position which Scripture holds. In doing this a Church runs the risk to which we have adverted, of seating herself on the Throne of God, and falling into the condemnation consequent thereon.

The claim put forward by the Roman Church to interpret Holy Scripture, is based upon a foundation which is delusive.

She rests her claim upon a commission of which she

herself, on her own principles, is the author. It is taken from Holy Scripture. But Holy Scripture, she says, is the voice of the Church, and she is the Church, she only. When any such commission is testified to by others than by Rome, as being contained in Holy Scripture, or when it is claimed by her, as tradition, apart from Scripture, they are either ignorant of its application to Rome or it is denied by them.

The office of the Church at large as to Revelation is introductory and conservative. Introductory, because when its object is accomplished it is no more needed. A teacher who has shown us a mathematical problem is no more requisite; it stands sufficient to us in its own strength. Nay, were he to attempt to disprove it, he would no longer be able to do so.

So it is with the Church and Scripture. The Church introduces Scripture and so teaches. When the Gospel is received, the teacher's office is ended. Such is the office of the Church as to Scripture. It is external as testimonial, limited as instructive. It is conservative likewise, handing down the words committed to her care as the pillar and ground of the truth. This is her office and her glory. She must not go beyond this. She is the receptacle and conveyance, not the source or stream. Revelation does not come *from* her, but *to* her; when she goes beyond this she seats herself on the throne of God. She is a witness, not a source. The distinction is fundamental. God is the author of Revelation, speaking in times past, to the fathers by the Prophets, and in these last days unto us by His Son. The summary of this address is conveyed in Holy Scripture. This is the cause, the effect is as we have already indicated. The end is obtained by the exercise and development of the faculties to which it is addressed, thus producing, by a Divine spirit, a new and higher life in the human soul. More than and other than this it cannot be. It is that which a child may compass, and yet where the philosopher may put himself but as the child gathering pebbles on the ocean's shore. It is a Divine life produced in a certain way; a simple following of its Great Head and Author. Christianity is to be that which Christ was when on earth. This is its end. Revelation is the means for accomplishing this end—Revelation received in the Spirit of Christ— the Divine Spirit. It cannot be but this, or other than this, for it cannot have anything it does not get from Him. It is the communication of a Divine life, through the manifestation of a Divine life. It is the Spirit, the power, the nature of Christ living and manifesting itself in us as it did in Him. It is the raising up of a Divine life in our souls, through the knowledge of the Divine life in the Son, the Spirit of the Son entering into our spirits, and we becoming sons also in our time and measure. Without Christ we can do nothing; all that we attain to is by the process of knowing Christ, and putting on Christ. 'I am the way, the truth, and the life,' He saith. That is the summary of it; we must know Christ and have Him in us, our hope and glory; we must know the power of His resurrection, and have fellowship in His sufferings, and conformity to His death. We must have righteousness, peace and joy in the Holy Ghost; not an outward but an inward Christ; nothing else will do us good, nothing else will save us. There must be an inward voice to which we ever answer, 'speak Lord, for thy servant heareth,' and with which we are one. This only is Christianity, Christianity and true wisdom. He that has this, has the key of all knowledge. He that has not this, has nothing. He that has this needeth no one to teach him, no evidence beyond. He knows in whom he believes, he has the evidence in himself; he may not be able to impart it; it is a name which no man knoweth, saving he who receiveth it, but he knows it; the secret of the Lord is with him, and were he to ignore, or refuse to confess it, in the solemn language of St. John, he would 'make God a liar.'

If Christianity is this, it lies in a small compass. It must be contained in a small casket. It is this; and it is contained in God's word. There we have the outline of it. The application is in our own lives, wrought out within us by the Holy Spirit. Now if God's word contains it, who shall say that it requires addition, whether by way of comment or interpretation? Who shall say that it ought to be more plain, or that it is not enough? Who will venture to make additions to it, or still more to make such needful for salvation, or for membership in Christ's Body?

Let us now draw some conclusions from what has been advanced, and to that end I would ask—had not every several Church made its own addition to the Word of God, it were too much to say that there would now have been but one Catholic Church? Had not the Roman Church, had not the Eastern, had not the Anglican, and the Scotch, and the Anabaptist, the Lutheran, Calvinist and other Churches not appended their own codicils to the Old and New Testament, would there now have been more than one communion among Christians? I think not.

I do not advocate the abolition of what are called Standards. I only would caution against their position being confounded with that of the Word of God, or from our being disquieted at different human interpretations.

At present many are alarmed by its being alleged, that by such interpretations as are sometimes made, Dogma is discarded.

But what is dogma? It cannot be anything beyond what is contained in God's Word. And if God's Word be not discarded, then is dogma not discarded. If by dogma is meant beyond what is in the Word of God, no doubt such dogma ought to be discarded.

In truth the late alarm has been caused (I speak myself as one who feels guilty) from our having been living on a lower spiritual level than we should have lived. Had we been living in the consciousness of God's light, we should not have demanded light from earthly sources, or have been confounded if we did not receive it. Such a cry for external guidance as we have lately heard, is it not the cry of Israel for a King, when the Lord was King?

Living in the light of God's presence, spiritual difficulties vanish away. In truth, no proof could be greater of our having erred from the way, and seeking after other than the true Guide and evidence, than the present cry for human definition. It is natural to think that human definitions strengthen; it is natural to lean on an arm of flesh, but it gives no real strength, it is no spiritual addition. Sometimes we seem as if we thought that our decisions actually created or altered a fact, or bound down Almighty God;—one presumption leading to another. Let us in this, as in all things, remember that we are but receivers, and that of His fulness we *have* received, and be content with such things as we have. Have we not His Word and Spirit? Are not His Word and Spirit enough?

Let us be strong in the strength of receiving the truth from them, and see light in this light. Truth is strong by its own strength, and not by the strength of others. Light is seen by its own light, and not by the light of others. Let us be in the light and conscious of it, and we are safe.

This is not the consciousness of having formed an opinion, but of receiving a new life, and receiving it ourselves. The light of others cannot be our light; the strength of others be our strength; the conviction of others our convictions. They must be our own, or they are nothing to us. If not our own, they are external, and unconnected; and as we live without them, we die without them. No man can believe save on his own conviction, and whether he derive this from others, in the way of going with the majority, or on supernatural, or other grounds, it is on his own conviction that he believes, if he believes at all; and no man believes without knowing that he believes. A true Christian faith or belief is to have a consciousness of a new life, a life which has its witness in itself—the witness that in Christ we have light, and that it *is* light. There is no true security or evidence but this—authorities may err, majorities are no test of truth; we are warned against false Christs and false miracles. The only security against false Christs is to know the true; no testimony to the truth is equal to the proof from its own power, and possibly this is the reason why miracles have been discontinued to the Church.

What we require at present, then, is not dogma, or mere definition, but eyes to see, and ears to hear that which we have—spirit, not letter—the Holy Spirit of God.

It is not theology we require; save the theology

which consists in things, not in distinctions. Too often theology is put in the place of God—knowing the title, not the nature, an useless and dangerous knowledge, for when this is lost, all is lost. Too often theology is but a hortus siccus of dead plants, of which the learned collector has the lifeless form, the unlearned gardener the bloom and beauty. Nor is it masters in Israel that are needed, but to know the truth every one for himself; as it is writen, 'they shall be all taught of God.' Calling men masters, we are apt to be as those watchmen of our houses—the dogs—which (when one sees a thief getting in at night), alarm by barking; and hearing him all the dogs in the village bark, while but one only saw the thief, and it may be, he saw nothing. So it is with us when we follow men, who may, or may not, know the truth. How great the confusion when these give the alarm at nothing.

One by one, as we came into the world, so one by one must we learn the truth, every one for himself; first the letter, then the spirit; first authority, then experience; there is no road but this. What really is wanted is, that all should know the truth—each one for himself, by having Holy Scripture interpreted by the Holy Spirit. Then only can we be led into spiritual truth, and the meaning of Revelation; but thus we are so *fully*. For thus we know, not only that Holy Scripture comes from God, but what it is that comes from Him. Thus we know that which is Holy Scripture, and that which is not. Thus we know the meaning of inspiration, and how far it goes. Thus we are able to sever the treasure from the earthern vessel; the human from the Divine element in Scripture; and this we shall do with a superhuman infallibility, for as the electric fluid runs through a substance enlightening that which is of its own nature, and passing over in darkness that which is not, so such an one in studying Holy Scripture will be kept from receiving that which is human in it, as if it were Divine, and that which is Divine as if it were human. The real want of the day and of the Church now is reliance on the Holy Spirit, realisation that this is the reign of the Spirit, and that nothing comes by human might or power in spiritual things, but solely by the Spirit of God. With the gift of the Holy Scripture, we yet shall come short of the truth, unless we take to Holy Scripture the spirit in which it was written, unless we see with the eyes of the Holy Spirit, and hear with His ears. Spiritual truth lies in a medium of its own, and although we may have it revealed, we do not discern it until we are attuned to it. This is that which is called being born of the Spirit; and to this I would call attention; for, saith St. Paul, 'What man knoweth the things of a man, save by the spirit of man which is in him? Even so knoweth no man the things of God, but (by) the Spirit of God.' And, again, 'Now we have received,' says he, 'not the Spirit of the world, but the Spirit which is of God, that we might know the things which are freely given to us of God;' 'for no man,' he concludes, 'hath known the mind of the Lord,' but 'by having the mind or Spirit of Christ.' Now the Holy Spirit is present, is ever present with the truth. He helpeth us (we read) with groanings which cannot be uttered, but we do not realise this, nor the need of His aid, nor the possibility of seeing spiritual truth alone by His assistance, and thus it is we are as we are. We seek defences of human wisdom, interpretations from a human source by human words, forgetting how valueless they are.

For if we can discern the sense of Holy Scripture by the aid of the Holy Spirit, is human interpretation to supersede that aid? Or, if the interpretation be true, do we not need the same Holy Spirit to interpret it, as we did to interpret the original from whence it was taken? And if it be false, what is its place?

Why require what is not necessary, and what may not be true, when all that is necessary, and which we know to be true, is already in our hands?

No Church having Holy Scripture, and the presence of the Holy Ghost, and the due administration of the Sacraments, can of necessity require more. And this no doubt will be granted, for we say that 'Holy Scripture containeth all things necessary for salvation.' Yet, so ready is man to put in his own word and require an arm of flesh, that no sooner is this said, even by Protestant Churches just delivered from Roman interpretations on the plea of private judgment, than they proceed to lay down interpretations of their own, as needful for their members.

Yet, no doubt, the question will arise, were Holy Scripture the sole standard of devotion, by what means would Churches be kept together?

We all know the variations of doctrine which have arisen, all equally claiming to be taken from Holy Scripture. How are we to deal with the teachers of different doctrines? The question will become a practical one in every locality.

But the real difficulty is, what can we substitute which may not lead into error? and what right have we to add anything to the Word of God?

And practically in England it has been as if Holy Scripture were the sole standard, since the difference between high and low Church doctrine (although in some respects great, as being not without some warrant on either side in Scripture) has been treated as if both were one.

Variations beyond this cannot fairly be said to be deduced from Scripture only.

The dilemma however is this, that we must either make Scripture the basis, or some standard beyond; and such may be unwarrantable and will be variable, with the variations of human opinion. This latter method has been that adopted heretofore, but the constant variation which has thus assuredly been created, by the setting aside of previous standards, is more dangerous to the faith at large than the changes or variations of opinion in individuals, appealing to the one and invariable standard of Holy Scripture. The decrees of the various councils with the exception of five are set aside by the Church of England. Almost all the leading Churches, she declares to have erred; she repudiates all Standards but her own necessarily; but who can tell how long these will be permanent?

At present a large number, discontented with a late decision, agitate for another Court, that they may obtain another verdict; were this obtained, the other party, equally discontented in its turn, would claim another Court, to get another hearing, both parties to end by making Standards of their own, when other means failed, and Standards which would vary with the variation of the parties in the Church.

So has it ever been, so will it be, where this system is pursued. Each claim of course to be the Church, and to have the truth, and as majorities cannot settle this, the contest is infinite, and the unsettlement of faith on this principle greater probably than on any other, greater assuredly than by leaving the Word of God alone, as the one Standard.

No doubt the variations of interpretation of Scripture by private judgment have been held forth as fatal to its claim to guidance; and Bossuet's argument is known to most. And the unity of interpretation of Scripture, and infallibility claimed by Rome in guidance, are her strength and argument of most importance in the present day.

It is to be considered however whether the variations of Protestantism are so destructive as is alleged. And whether it is possible to possess truth in any way, than by enquiry—truth, that is, as set forth in Revelation, where the principle is plain, that truth is to be sought after to be found. Assuredly, under any other system than one of enquiry, it is more than doubtful whether the possession of truth without enquiry is possession at all. Knowledge is essential to knowing, and without enquiry there is no knowledge of God in the sense of Revelation and its fruits. Is the knowledge of God acquired by others, and summed up in a formula, supposing it to be correct, sufficient? Is it our own knowledge? Do we know God or the formula merely? Is not a formula which maintains external unity more expressive of death than life? Where there is no experience, can there be spiritual life? Is there faith, where there is no reason for faith? The variations of Protestantism indicate enquiry and life, and are to be looked upon rather as the expression of various stages of spiritual growth in individuals and nations, than as the attainment of ultimate truth, and such variation (with the exception of Unitarianism, which does not obtain, where Scripture is held to be only understood, by the influence of the Holy Spirit,—and which likewise is on the wane) is not so destructive to what is of importance to the Faith, as is sometimes supposed. What is called the general orthodoxy, or concurrence in fundamentals of Protestant Churches, is remarkable, while limitation of expression as in Rome, where it cannot be the expression of experience, and is necessarily confined, is fatal to enquiry, and must be productive of spiritual death. It is indeed productive of an aberration of life, which is nearly as detrimental as death itself, in the acceptance of lower forms of spiritual attainment than those given by Revelation, as for example the worship of Saints and Angels, of the human Mother of our Lord, and of times and places especially beneficial.

If we judge a tree by its fruits, if the variations developed by enquiry have slain their thousands, the spiritual death engendered by limitation and its consequent false outgoings have slain their ten thousands, as those who know the countries where it reigns cannot refuse to testify. But indeed, if the knowledge of God is requisite for salvation, and if salvation is based on that knowledge for the attainment of its consummation, 'fellowship with the Father,' no limitation or system which aims mainly at definition can supply the want required. An Ark is not sufficient if the beasts within remain unclean.

No doubt much of our present difficulty arises from an unauthorised restriction of the meaning of the term, 'the faith once (for all) delivered to the Saints.' This is generally supposed to mean, that the faith was once for all delivered in Judea by God unto the faithful there. And this is true, if we mean that what was done there contained the faith and was done once for all—the record of which we have in Holy Scripture;

but it is not true if we suppose that the meaning of that was known there once for all, and conveyed down to us. We have Holy Scripture which conveys this, and is itself invariable, but its sense and meaning are but gradually developed as time runs on, and much of its meaning is hidden to the present hour. It is as yet ahead of all interpretations of it. The Prophets searched diligently for the meaning of that which they spake, but they did not (we read) always find it. The meaning of prophecy is seldom discovered until after the utterance itself; the declarations in the Apocalypse can only find their meaning with the lapse of ages. St. Paul testifies that the salvation in Jesus, in its fulness, will only be understood in after time. The Church was to be led into all truth by the Holy Ghost. The fulfilment of this promise it is which throws light on Scripture, and gives us the meaning to the things which Jesus did, and the fulness which in Him liveth, age by age as is required. But it cannot be limited to times and seasons, but must go on continually, and increasingly. The past facts of Revelation remain the same, the Holy Land and its inhabitants and Scripture are unaltered, but the light, the Holy Spirit, is not past but present, and is ever increasing in brightness as experience and time run on. Scripture itself is always ahead of and greater than the illumination of the time, howbeit the illumination groweth.

Let us distinguish however what this illumination is, and its true and false aspects. The doctrine of increase of light is held by the Church of Rome, and is called development, and is important and would be beneficial were it not confused by her fundamental error that Revelation comes from the Church, instead of going to the Church, and from the Church as a body instead of from individuals to the Church,—individuals speaking by the Holy Ghost.

It is plain that the Prophets and the Apostles, and the first Preachers of the Gospel, spake not for the Church of their time, but to it. It is so always. The Church has, as a whole, given no such illumination, no doctrinal utterance. At Jerusalem even, she confined herself to points of discipline. And of the general councils, and utterances of particular Churches, we receive but few, and they become increasingly difficult to those who receive them all. Individuals born of the Spirit for this purpose, Athanasius, Augustin, Luther, by such instruments as these it is that the increasing light is given, and the interpretation and illumination of Scripture groweth. By these and by Providential teaching in nature and in man.

As the time rolls on we see great light thrown upon Creation, past epochs, many systems of worlds added to our view; the Lord and Giver of Life, the Holy Spirit of God we see around and within us, in divers manners, and various ways which were unknown to our fathers. In these varieties of operation, however, it is the same Spirit, and we take His light to His written word, and read it by it. If that great light shews more of human adaptation in the written page than we expected, we bow the head and say, Let God be true, the God of nature and of Revelation is one God. Hear O Israel.

Forgetting that the light comes to the Church, not from the Church, the Roman Church, as we know, stretched forth her hand Jeroboam-like to Galileo revealing light, and has never been able to draw it back again. Confounding herself and Scripture at one blow. Let us read the warning. Let us understand that

## PRESENT STATE OF RELIGION.     35

while the faith was delivered once for all in Holy
Scripture, the light to see it by, the spirit and the
truth, are not bound up with it but outside of it, light-
ing it with increasing light, as time and the world rolls
on ; and doing so most often by gifts given to individuals.

There is nothing like end or death in Revelation,
it is life and peace, the robust life and peace of
enquiry.

But it may be felt that such a view of religion as
requires search and understanding on the part of every
man, is quite unfitted for the great majority of human
beings, who merely require, or can only have, a religion
of obedience, and simple comprehension. And this is
true, but it still remains and is first of all to be considered, whether the Revelation in Scripture is other
than it has been set forth above, and whether this (if
properly conveyed) is not sufficiently simple ; and
finally, whether, if it had been truly conveyed, Christendom would be as it is, and has been. It is at
least a question whether or not the *non*-conveyance of
the Gospel of enquiry, and so of 'fellowship with the
Father through the Son,' has not been the means of
Christendom being as it is, and as it has been; whether
Revelation being such as it is, and being given for the
express purpose of elevating humanity, humanity has not
been elevated precisely because the proper means have
not been adopted; whether the notion of its requiring
sense and understanding, and so being quite unfitted
for the great majority of human beings, who only
require a religion of obedience, and simple comprehension, and so something supposed to be this, being
given instead of Revelation (as we have described it)—
has not been the cause of humanity being left as it has

been, and Christendom being as it is, and the people remaining without sense and understanding. Such an idea (as another Gospel) could not have emanated from any one really acquainted with, and under the influence of Revelation, because such an one is sure that nothing but knowledge of, and communion with God through Christ, is the meaning of Revelation, and can save. But unfortunately many who are teachers do not seem to know this, and so not knowing it, act according to their own light, teaching what they think most likely to do good, or to be suitable; a false and esoteric system,—a region of darkness, producing darkness—blind leaders, leading to blindness.

If Revelation is addressed to every man, the question must be brought to the issue set forth in the Epistles of St. John and St. Paul, where the eternal or Divine Life is arrogated to be obtained alone by knowledge of God and Jesus Christ, so that 'whoso hath the Son hath life, and whoso hath not the Son hath not life.' Whether it is open to take any other or lower ground, or whether any other but the appointed means will produce the right result, we need not ask.

To those who know the truth, the simplicity of Revelation as contained in knowing the Father through the Son (and working that knowledge out as it is intended by God we should work it out through the providences of daily life), as it is the only method which can elevate and bless mankind, so is it the most easy and the most applicable to all conditions. It is so plain that he who reads the Scriptures or hears them read in the Holy Spirit cannot miss their meaning, and our daily life secures that its application be experienced. Yet what power have not the rulers of the darkness of this world to prevent this being known, and to substitute something in its place, and this not only in non-Protestant countries, but in those which have the Scriptures! Theologies making that obscure which is most simple, and mere moralities and substitutions of privilege coming between the Gospel and its end.

But besides, do not human definitions and summaries tend to take rank with the Scriptures, until in many countries they are substituted for the Scriptures? Are not whole countries without the word of God? Having but summaries and substitutes for Scripture, and having been so for a thousand years, can we wonder that Christendom is as it is? The great majority of nominal Christians having never seen or having never heard the Word of God! knowing nothing of it, because of human definitions and summaries which have taken its place, what is the consequence but that they are worshippers (if they do worship) not of the God of Revelation but of the substitution which has taken His place, even as the human definition has taken the place of Scripture? Worshippers of Angels and of Saints, and of the human Mother of our Lord!

Oh! do we realise that there are whole kingdoms called Christian which have never seen the Word of God —Christians who have had the Word of God taken from them to be replaced by human definitions; definitions which have found place from admission of the fundamental error, that truth comes from the Church instead of to the Church. If there is to be loss from variation or interpretation of God's Word when interpreted by the Spirit of God, as there is loss assuredly when aught is substituted for it, should we not say with David 'Let me fall into the hand of God and not into the hand of man.'

But this is not all. Let human definitions or interpretations be put into the place of the Word of God, human nature, bearing witness to itself, will speedily assert its own kingdom. The flesh will subdue the spirit, and the fruit will be in accordance with the seed. To human definitions of the word, human sacrifices are offered, and Italy and Spain, Piedmont, Flanders, France, English Smithfield and other places, St. Bartholomew and other days, have heard their cries. Having zeal, but not according to knowledge; thinking to do God service, they turn an angel into Satan—the Word of God into tradition. How grievous is the change, how different the principle in Holy Scripture, when fire was to be called from Heaven on those who would not hear. The Lord rebukes, and says 'Ye know not what spirit ye are of,' 'Overcome evil with good,' but the human spirit cries (meaning perhaps well after its light) 'Away with Him, crucify Him; better that one man suffer, that a whole nation perish not.'

And yet a woe remaineth. Putting that which is incomprehensible into the room of the comprehensible, an abstract assertion into the place of the instruction and reasoning of the Word of God, what follows but this, that men are unable to believe where there is no reason for faith to receive, assertion being at variance with understanding and conscience. The substitutions which are placed in room of Holy Scripture produce not faith but infidelity. Nowhere is infidelity so common and so real, among the intelligent, as in those countries where tradition is substituted for the Word of God; and among the unintelligent, where faith is a substitution, and has taken the place of faith in the Word of God, of what value is it? Such faith brings no one nearer unto God. It gives no knowledge no understanding of, and no conformity to God, whereby only cometh health and salvation. How deeply pathetic it is to see

<blockquote>Upon saints and angels spent the love which should be thine;</blockquote>

and to behold clasped hands, clasped most earnestly, and held up to things which cannot profit! On such no doubt God the Father looks down with pity; but with what emotions can He look on those who seek to bring nations and individuals to this condition, and that too after such experience as the world has had of this system. How can He look on those who take away the key of knowledge, and make the Word of God of none effect, by their traditions?

And it has been sought, yea, and now is, to reduce England to this condition! to lower England to this level! Surely may it not be said that our fathers have laboured in vain, and spent their strength for nought,—have suffered so many things in vain? Having been made free, do *we* seek to return to bondage; having been called to the liberty of sons, do *we* desire the condition of servants?

Unquestionably at this moment there is peril in the path of the Church of England. Looking at the indications of the mind of her ministers and members, displayed in such a manner as we can gather from the titles of books, and of other publications, we cannot but observe that the future is fraught with peril. For example, in the advertisements of the 'Guardian' newspaper, there is an evident seeking for issue on other principles than those of the Church of England; of dissatisfaction, and desire for union with persons and principles from which the Church of England has secured herself in times past; and from whom she kept aloof with a holy reticence as being in error, if not in sin. That newspaper itself cannot be said to favour such a movement, nay it does, with singular fairness and increasing earnestness, endeavour to do justice to all parties within the Church, and by so doing deserves great honour, and retains a place which otherwise it would not occupy; but apart from this, and judging by the tone of its advertisements and correspondence, we must discern a peril in the future to which no overseer of the Church should blind himself.

We see an increasing tendency on the part of those who recognise not the sufficiency of Scripture, and the Holy Spirit, to listen to the voice of Rome, to take her shorter path, and already too many have heard her call. In years not long gone by there was a large secession, which late events threaten to revive amongst us, and forms which had become spectral, and voices which had become echoes, are heard around, beckoning us to a bankrupt peace, and to an emasculated humanity. Well-known and not unhonoured forms over whom England mourns. Are they really better than they were? That 'kindly light,' when they possessed it, was it not the true light? Assuredly it was. Alas! now they say we see not light, save by the light of others,—know not God's light, know not God's voice, save by the light and voice of others, save it is on a particular candlestick, and save it comes from a particular place. Alas! must they not also say, they know not, if even they know this?—that if they know not anything aright themselves, they know not if they know anything at all? Such confusion must await on all who put out the eyes which God has given them.

And with theirs is heard a voice we would gladly honour for the word he spake, 'It has been one longing of my life, that those who love the Lord Jesus Christ in sincerity should be drawn together.' A voice we would gladly honour for this, and other things, but now when mingled with that of those who have shaken the tree of life in England and have cast down some of its fairest fruit, we cannot honour when heard again in the same direction. Alas! how many of fair daughters and brave sons have these voices taken from their mother,—who have now crossed that bourne and Rubicon whence no traveller returns;—whom, in our most illustrious homes, our English Rachel mourns. Surely that is now the voice of the 'false mother' when it counsels the division of the Church of England. Alas! must we not try the spirits and hold fast alone that which is good? When we hear this voice give such counsel, and when we hear it speak against our highest dignity in judicature, that it is 'the unjust judge' of Scripture,—a court and country the purest and most free among the nations, we must resist such voice, were it an Apostle's, when it is to be blamed.

And what do they do who by their private judgment judge, and leave the Church of England? Condemning private judgment! Do they consider how their acts affect the general aspects of religion, and the progress of the Word of God, especially amongst those churches to which the apostles first conveyed it, and the Roman in particular? Do they know the fact that not only of the laity, but of the clergy, many dissatisfied and hungering after God within those Churches, believing that there is more to know than they have known, and that more is known than what they know, and doubting that the premises must be wrong which age after age (however logically yet surely falsely) in a descending ratio separates them further from, instead of bringing them nearer unto God, and who feeling their emptiness, their 'sighing and having nothing,' were turning their eyes to England, not without hope that that great country, the model and the refuge of the nations in civil things, might be their help and refuge likewise in their religious things, but who now seeing those reputed to be doctors in the Church of England straggling towards themselves, have ceased to look and hope?

Are these enquirers and hopeful souls convinced by such a sight that they themselves were right before? Alas! they knew all that they had before, and that it satisfied not. Do those priests who have left the Church of England consider what they have done to such souls as these? The conclusion they come to is (in the Athenian's words) this, 'all that we know is, nothing can be known.' And who is answerable for this but those priests of the Church of England, who hindered them who were seeking the truth and were entering in, when they took away the key of knowledge. And have they themselves been welcomed where they went? (I speak still of the English priesthood)—are they not distrusted as strangers and foreigners, put on one side as doubtful or vulgar friends? They who were in their own England the respected pastors of respected flocks, and the head of quiet homes, where God's Word was ever by the hearth and on the altar. What are they now?

But we must consider the question from a higher ground. We are told that it is an age of scepticism; that infidelity is coming in like a flood; and that dogma alone can save us. What are the facts? What are the signs of this scepticism and infidelity?

Ours is an age of thought and progress: of earnestness and sagacity; of revelation of and enquiry into nature on every hand. The same spirit has been extended to questions of religion, endeavours are made to reconcile Revelation with the progress of science and civilization, demands are made for information as to the meaning of Revelation. It is not a denial of its truth or divine origin that we hear; at least it was not, and we trust it may not degenerate to that. The cry has been to be brought nearer unto God, to know more of God and of the connection of His written word with His works in nature. If this be scepticism it differs from the scepticism of all previous ages, in that it is not desirous to discover that religion (as revealed in Scripture) is false, but that it is true. It is the cry of children, their cry for food, for food 'convenient for them.'

He greatly misreads, as I conceive, the signs of the times who supposes it is infidelity which is at work. It may become so, but it is not so as yet. Never was there a stronger desire on the part of man to find the footsteps of God. How to supply the want is another question. That dogma or mere assertion will do so is more than doubtful. 'It is milk' (let it be said), not strong meat, which is required; a reason for the faith, increase in the knowledge of God, to know *what* men worship, that they *may* worship in spirit and in truth. And assuredly, if ignorance is the mother of devotion, it is not a devotion well pleasing unto Him who bids those who worship know *what* they worship. Yea, if there is infidelity abroad, may it not be asked, is it not caused by a want of fitting nourishment, by giving our little ones stones for bread, hard assertions, dogmatic summaries, and nailing up conventionalities of which the writing cannot be read, but by reading it 'backwards like a Hebrew Book,' and saying as was said to Galileo, 'it must not be,' while yet it was so. Well spake the abbé Ventura when he said, 'if the Church keeps not pace with the world, the world will go beyond and turn round and teach her.' Let us take heed, lest our place be taken from us. The Church made her great progress at first by being before the world, and by giving higher truths, further insight into nature and into grace, so only can she keep herself a-head of the world, to the end of time.

Let us be sure that truth can alone be dangerous to error, that the works and word of God, if rightly understood, are one; that we do not help the word by disowning the teaching of the works, or by drawing a line and saying, 'hitherto shalt thou come and no further, and here thy proud waves be stayed.' In this we shall show but our own ignorance, and our own presumption. God, who gave us Holy Scripture, gives us also nature; and on that which is fixed and unchangeable, Scripture throws His light variably and increasingly as the world rolls on, as mankind requires and as nature becomes developed. Thus is He with us to the end of time,—the teacher and expounder of His word. The Spirit is not confined to the past, dead in the letter of Scripture, but free and living, and present always, transforming the letter by the Spirit, converting the history of the past into the experience of the present, and shining with increasing light, and teaching with increasing clearness, as night and morning pass into the perfect day.

When the conventional pictures of the Byzantine School were being superseded in churches by paintings taken from life, the ancients stigmatised the modern painters as heretical and infidel; the modern the ancients, as absurd and idolatrous. It is a lesson for ourselves. Let us not stamp the Scriptures with our own measurements, applying the measure of a man to the word of God; nor print the great ocean sand with human footsteps and say they are Divine. With the words of Holy Scripture we have enough; they are sufficient; yea, it is akin to blasphemy to ask for more. Let us not fear,—there *is* nought to fear but the presumption which would reduce them and limit them by human interpretation. The definitions of the past could not be again repeated; the definitions of the past would not be made by us. Assuredly there is an upward progress. Would an assembly of Divines again convened at Westminster draw out what is called the 'Westminster Confession?' Did not the American Episcopate but the other day omit the creed of Athanasius, and that not in dissenting from the Catholic faith therein contained, but from the mode by which it is therein limited and defined. Is not the Church of England at one with her American sister, or sees no ground of difference in this?

But, in fine, it will be said that Scripture no doubt is sufficient when taught by the Holy Spirit; but that the difficulty is as to the *mode* by which the Spirit operates; whether it is on the Church collectively, or on the individual. If, as we learn from a recent good authority (Newman's 'Apology,' p. 395), the Church has given but one new decision in 800 years, and has authoritatively spoken but once in every century since her origin, of what value is such operation to the individual? In the study of Holy Scripture, next to none. If, then, the promise of the gift of the Spirit has been fulfilled, it must be by acting on the individual. From this there is no outlet, for if it be held that the Church is only guided as a whole into truth, then guidance to the individual is denied; and yet as truth is alone learnt of the Spirit, he who has learnt it (even in the Church of Rome) must have done so by the Spirit teaching the individual. But experimentally there is no difficulty; he who has been taught has the witness of the teaching in himself, and to deny or ignore this would be, not humility or modesty, but sin against the Holy Ghost. Let us believe, that the simplest must be the surest method, and take that which brings us most near unto God, and makes us lean upon the naked arm of Jehovah; and that, assuredly, is the Holy Spirit dealing with us individually.

No doubt, by a class which is still very large, the doctrine of 'Scripture and the Spirit' is looked upon as a delusion, a form of words, or a begging of the question; and assuredly the Holy Spirit has not occupied the place which He ought to have occupied in connection with the reception of the meaning of Holy Scripture in most minds; and to this may probably be attributed much of the darkness and imperfection of the past. But the reign of the Spirit presses on, and cannot but assume ere long the position which it ought.

That God has revealed Himself in His Word, we all, more or less, grant, but that we do not understand this Revelation without the Holy Spirit's aid, is not so generally granted. Yet it must be so; for I think that most will grant that unless we have some of that spirit in which a book is written, we do not enter into the meaning of the book.—that unless our spirit is attuned to a melody, we do not enter into its power;—that without a musical ear, music to us is nought. Now this assuredly is true of Scripture as of other things, and in a higher sense as Scripture reaches to higher matters. That attuning is the act of the Spirit or the presence of the Spirit in the individual.

The removing of the Holy Spirit from dealing individually to dealing collectively with mankind, however little men may mean it, is nothing less than removing God to a distance, and living without His presence; and were such the teaching only of those who wish to make this the case, it would be evident from what source such inspiration comes, but as in general this is not intended, we can only conclude it to be a logical necessity from unsound premises—from the unsound premises that there must be an infallible external and human direction over and above that of Holy Scripture. On no other supposition is it possible to explain such a position as that laid down, for example, but the other day in a 'Letter to the "Times" on the New Court of Appeal,' by one of the most esteemed clergymen of our Church, when he says, that the thirty-nine Articles and all authoritative decisions emanating from our Church, are made under an expressed or virtual appeal to an Ecumenical Council when such can be had.* Is not this to separate us from God, and from all positive and actual belief? Nay, what is this but to deprive us of all real belief? Do we believe, or can we believe, if our belief is contingent on the decree of some future assembly? Are we not

* Mr. Keble's Letter to the 'Times.'

to know, do we not know God, but through such a medium, which is indeed no medium, for it may never be, or we may never know of it? If our knowledge of God depends on such means as these, then, indeed, are Christians of all men most miserable, for they may believe it is true, but if an Ecumenical Council afterwards forbid, they are to let their belief go! They are to believe, as it were, under protest. 'I believe in the Holy Trinity,' but only as dependent on the after decision of an Ecumenical Council. Is such a thing possible? Can human wisdom and prudence remove us farther from a child-like belief in God than this? Surely, we should call no man master, and we should take heed lest the instrumentality which is given to bring us nearer to God, be not made the means of putting us farther from Him. And such, no doubt, would be the effect of removing the guidance or teaching of the Holy Spirit from the individual.

Holy Scripture contains the truth, but the truth is not vital to us unless we receive it in the Holy Spirit. Scripture and the Spirit are both required; singly or apart they are not sufficient. We must have Revelation, and we must have power to apprehend it. Both must act together in us. With both we are infallibly guided; alone they are insufficient. We can see that this is the case by examples taken from opposite quarters; from those, for instance, of the sect of Friends or Quakers, and those of the school of what is termed Pure Criticism. In the first case, the Spirit, held apart from the letter, but guides those who hold this doctrine into a vague generality; in the latter, the letter held apart from the Spirit has but a dead language. Each party possesses an element of power, and that which it contains, it gives (such force has even dislocated truth); but the result is imperfect. Its two necessary powers being put together, they would have attained, and do attain, their end; the end, that is, of Revelation, —the bestowal of a Divine life. Let us sum up and conclude this consideration.

The Spirit alone will not do, we must have what is called objective knowledge; a landscape for the Spirit to enlighten, a painting on the lamp, which the light shines through to illumine. The Scriptures alone are insufficient, the landscape, the painting, are not enough without the light. Both are needed, and when together make perfect. Both are ours. First the Scriptures; in them we have the objective truth—nowhere else so surely, nowhere else *originally*; for all that Christians have of Revelation is taken from Holy Scripture; all that we know of the early Church is found therein, all other writings are but echoes of it—so far as they are not they are profitless and false. It is the possession of it, and the truths therein contained which constitutes the teaching of the Church, and such Churches as lose or hide this knowledge are fallen Churches, the gates of hell have prevailed against them, they are no longer living branches of the true vine—the Church Catholic. They who keep the Scriptures have the truth and stand. But we must have the Spirit; without the Spirit objective truth is dead. But the Spirit is given to all.

With Scripture and the Holy Spirit we are safe: safe if we have both, and do not put asunder what God has joined together. Then we attain the end of Revelation, a Divine life, which is the product of truth, and the Divine Spirit. Without these two it is impossible for man to attain it, for no stream can rise above its source, no tree but be according to its root, and a

D

human root and source are not enough. With *this* root and with *this* fountain we can rise to a life beyond our own, a life akin to the Divine.

But I am reminded that the real risk to the truth and to the Church of England is not from holding over strongly the authority of Revelation or its supports : that the danger is from an opposite quarter. And no doubt the future is fraught with peril from that side; but at present I think the risk is on the other. On the side of an exaggeration, that is, not of the importance of Scripture, but of the place of authority in connection with it as its warrant, or its substitute. And this risk no doubt late events have encreased.

To this risk, they to whom these words are mainly addressed,—the younger clergy,—are, as I think, peculiarly exposed. They have not had sufficient time properly to experience truth on its own witness, and they naturally and no doubt righteously are guided by those whose names are venerable in the special circle in which clergy move.

In time the practical work of the ministry will diminish this risk, but till then we cannot but feel that peril is involved, and that it is the duty of the Church's spiritual overseers to caution their younger clergy against it. We dread lest the younger clergy may enter on a dangerous road under insufficient knowledge, or may suddenly place themselves in a false position. Once really engaged in the cure of souls, and we think the risk is passed. Once engaged in the real work of the Christian ministry, and away from the dilettante theology of those who have no such corrective to their views, and who are more conversant with the past than with the present, and they will be safe we

## PRESENT STATE OF RELIGION. 51

think; but until then it behoves the overseers of Christ's Church to watch over them with anxiety. Once in the cure of souls, we say, in the midst of a groaning and travailing world, amongst sights and sounds of sin and sorrow, on the one hand; and on the other among young fresh lives and innocent children, they are not likely to abandon the vineyard of their mother, for any fanciful or unreal reason, because it has a 'Monophysite aspect.' If they hear such words they will hear also, 'What is that to thee, follow thou me.' Or they will think of the parable of the good Samaritan, and strive to realise what the Saviour of men would say to them, did He meet them abandoning the field on such an argument.

Such thoughts we hope may serve to check hasty resolutions. Would they were sufficient to bring back those who are gone. But besides the younger clergy, we think that at present another class and sex is in danger. There is risk at present we believe to the female sex. Constituted as the female mind is 'to be under authority,' authority has great and proper claims to its regard, and a theology which bases itself upon it has many attractions for it, and no theology perhaps in which it is not prominent will be very seductive. To such, 'direction' is ever welcome and in some sense is proper. But the very excellencies of the female character expose it to danger from a theology which overvalues spiritual authority, and particularly when that authority is united to the attractions of good works, devotional observances, and external beauty. To this must be added at present another risk. The argument for authority, when gainsaid, has a tendency to make its votaries deem themselves injured along with their principles, and to class themselves among the

D 2

martyrs and confessors of religion—alas! too common. How many, both in Churches and in families, have offered themselves at this sad altar, destroying themselves and disturbing others. Such martyrdoms, however, taken for true, call out the sympathy and generous devotion of the female mind, and add another to the perils at present threatening.

The risk to the female sex and to the younger clergy at present is great we believe, and mainly from the very excellencies of both these parties. There is yet one peril to be observed in this quarter which ought to be guarded against. That which arises from an assumption that human authority can settle some of the present difficulties of Religion. Those who hold this view of authority or what may be termed 'the Roman Theology,' would settle as they conceive, and silence all opposition, by a scoff at the result produced by a non-adoption of their mode of treatment. Let us take the strong and prominent example at present before us. An English missionary lately sent to convert the heathen, and who returned (as they allege) converted by them, is blamed because he did not 'settle the question by authority.' Had that been done (it is said), no such result as has taken place could have resulted from it. But could this have been done, could it so have been settled? On the contrary, had this been attempted, not only would no better result have followed, but an infinitely worse, for faith and honesty themselves would have been put to hazard. Unsatisfactory and mistaken as was the course, we think, which the missionary adopted, it was incomparably preferable to that which was suggested, or that to which the Roman Theology must have had recourse. The method adopted did not answer the objections of the adversaries; nay, it left them under the impression that less could be said for the boasted religion of civilization than had been expected. Still something was gained; it left at least an impression that truth and honesty were of value. But had the other course been adopted, not only no satisfaction on the points in controversy would have resulted, but truth and religion would have been overthrown together. Let us remember the objections taken, and observe what (on the Roman Theology) the answers must have been, the mere objections taken to portions of the Pentateuch, for example—to creation having been accomplished in six of our days; discrepancies as to numbers; as to the sun going round the earth. And what must have been the Roman answer? It must have been, these are the truths, the Church says, and ever has said, so. These words are guaranteed by her infallibility. On Monday the light; on Tuesday the water; on Wednesday the land and trees; on Thursday the sun, moon, and stars were made, and so on throughout the chapter. And so, again, that the numbers do not tally is no error, the sun does go round the earth, the Church has said so. Nay (they might have added), farther, a modern Prelate of our own informs us that the sun is sixty miles from the earth and about the size of Drogheda, and the calculations ought to be in accordance; nevertheless for convenience sake we use the almanack. Such or something such must have been the answers given by the Roman Theology. And with what result? The satisfaction of the objector? Nay, would not everything have been put to hazard. Verily such answer would not have been in accordance with truth; the truth as they knew it. And such answer could not have been well pleasing to God. We may depend upon it that he who plays false with the earthly things he knows, will not be led into the truth concerning the Heavenly things he knows not,—that he that is unjust as to the things which are his own, will not be trusted with those which are another man's,—that he who is unjust in little, is unjust in much, and can be no scribe instructed in the kingdom of Heaven.

But the risk run to truth and to the Church of England from the opposite quarter is probably greater than that to which we have been adverting. Authority elevated out of its due place (in connection with Revelation) can always be shown to be in a false position by pressing the consequences which follow from its usurpation to their legitimate conclusion. Nothing can more clearly show this, than such an admission as that indicated in a late publication in behalf of the Church of Rome (Manning's letter to Dr. Pusey, 1864, p. 14), where after declaring that the Church is essential to salvation, and that the Roman is that Church, it concludes that it is often physically and morally impossible to judge a question so far removed from the primary truths of conscience and Christianity, as to which is the true Church or Revelation.

More than this cannot be requisite to show to what false conclusions the illegitimate use of authority leads; for it is evident from the above, either that the Church contended for cannot be *the* Church, or that no Church is requisite at all,—requisite, that is, for that salvation which 'the wayfaring man though a fool is not to err in;' into which but as little children we may not enter, and which is called emphatically a Gospel for the poor.

A Church which is 'far removed from the primary truths of conscience and Christianity' cannot be the Church of God spoken of in Scripture, but something the product of art and man's device; a human thing growing up from earth to heaven, not descending from Heaven to earth; a false thing erecting itself on the throne of God: authority, in short, usurping the place of truth, to be testified, and corrected in due time.

Authority exalted out of its due place may do harm for a time, but eventually is self-destructive; nevertheless when we see it thus, or fear its usurpation, we must be on our guard against it.

But no doubt the difficulties which impend over truth and the Church of England are greater on the other side, and will eventually be found more difficult to deal with; on the side, that is, which instead of attributing to authority a false and undue importance, concludes that there is no authority; no authority that is sufficient to authenticate Revelation; and no sufficient means of ascertaining its truth: a large and growing sentiment with which the future is dark.

What is the solution of this difficulty? The answer to this question? The supply to needs such as these? The want which has its root in the Athenian cry, 'All that we know is that nothing can be known?' In seeking an answer, let us take care that we neither trifle with truth, nor our own convictions: nor take a light view of their needs who are in want.

The answer is not one of mere assertion, nor can it be given in stereotyped expressions. The old 'order changeth giving place to new,' and can only be built up with fresh materials. We must stand on the same ground the objector stands on, to see what he sees, and to answer so that he can hear. We must use the words of understanding and reason. From not doing this, and from a false zeal for religion, 'a zeal not according to knowledge,' there is great risk of severing religion from the thought and progress of mankind; a severance which has taken place for many years in Southern Europe, where worship has been divorced from knowledge; a severance which there is some risk may be accomplished to some extent amongst ourselves.

We believe that the answer is the same as that to the other party, and that the need will be supplied in the same way; viz. by Revelation: Revelation as contained in Holy Scripture, received in the power of the Holy Ghost.

This however may be felt to be a begging of the question, an assumption of the point which is at issue. But in truth it is not so. So many hindrances have come in the way (in the way of Scripture being fairly tried), that we do not think that it is an assumption of the question to propose its sufficiency.

So many misconceptions as to Scripture have existed and do exist, so many misinterpretations of it, so little is made of the Holy Spirit as its interpreter to individuals, that we do not think the means have been sufficiently tried or recognised, so as to warrant any one in saying that they are not sufficient, or that it begs the question to assert them to be so. Many countries, professing Christianity, do not, properly speaking, possess the Bible; in many places strange substitutions have taken the place of its doctrines. In others its scope and spirit have been so strangely changed that the primitive meaning of Scripture is scarcely recognisable or represented. Let any one go to Milan, for example, and look at the picture of the Last Supper by Leonardo da Vinci, as it was at Jerusalem, and then into the cathedral, and see in the High Mass its present interpretation.

How many nations and individuals separate Revelation from common life; yea, separate religion from morality, and think that they can be, and (in some sort) ought to be separated. Thus we find monks and nuns called 'the Religious,' and in England a man is said, on becoming a clergyman, to 'go into the church,'—and elsewhere pious frauds are committed and defended,—and elsewhere the morality of Heaven made arbitrary! The things which it was given to obviate have been put into the place of Revelation, yea, have been supposed to be its production. These and similar causes have prevented Revelation from being fairly tried, and from having its due force, and from being recognised as containing the spiritual help we need. Rightly received, we believe it to be all that is required; of course, it must be rightly received. We must have it in its integrity, and have it rightly interpreted, but with this we shall have all that is required. This answer and supply, no doubt, limits itself to those who use it, but (as we have before said) the direction is sufficient, for as they who are in earnest and seek, will find, and find all they need; so to those who do not seek no direction is necessary. We doubt if there is any other than the way of search.

They who take this answer will find what they need, and in finding, will obtain a proof also of its authenticity, and not only so, but that the provision is inexhaustible; —that Scripture is not left behind by human progress, —that it is ever ahead of humanity, of humanity in its highest developement. No progress is perfect without Revelation; there is no real civilisation but that which comes out of it; no other voice direct from heaven; no other assurance of eternal life. In the light there given, a light is seen which requires no other witness, no external proof of its truth. Light indeed is ever its own witness, it can have no other; that which requires other manifestation is not light.

They who go where Scripture takes them, know whence it comes : as it lifts them above, it must come from above. The things which it reveals they know, and the region into which it takes them, with a knowledge and assurance to which other knowledge and other assurance are not to be compared. But, no doubt, there is a class which feels that the objections to Scripture are so patent, and its origin so unlikely, that without some irresistible proof, they will not yield themselves to the experiment of its operation. To these it is usual to offer such external proofs as History, Analogy, and Nature afford ; there are many such, and we believe them sufficient for their purpose. But we think that such proofs as are nearest to those derived from the internal powers of Scripture itself are more to be relied on, and are those most likely to be of the greatest use, especially at this moment. Let us look at some of these.

None, perhaps, are more valuable than those derived from the existence of the Christian life.

The Christian life is a reality, peculiar and specific. It is derived from a belief of the facts recorded in Revelation. Is it possible that the life should be real, and the facts out of which it is derived unreal?

The life could not have given birth to the facts, for they were anterior to it ; nor could the peculiarity of the facts have given birth to the life without their having a supernatural origin. For no other origin is possible if we consider them in their isolation, and, at the same time, connection ; in their being based on the assumption in many cases of a Divine origin, and other origin being impossible, if the facts are true. The facts have a testimony beyond gainsaying, if testimony is to be at all received. Again, a history extended over so great and varied a series of time and space, involving people and countries unconnected with one another, save in this way; and, on the other hand, *so* connected, that the alleged facts and that which flows from them, the laws and customs of a people, are otherwise inexplicable. A particular Nation seemed to exist (up to a certain epoch) but for the conservation of this knowledge, and now it seems to exist but to testify to its truth.

But further, as the ideas of truth and righteousness both among the Jews and in Christian writings are exalted to a higher place and obligation than ever they were before, or are seen elsewhere in the history of the world, they and their authors believed, at least, the truth of the facts to which they testify; and in many cases they sealed their belief in their testimony with their blood—their belief in the facts recorded in Scripture. It is scarcely possible, in the face of all this, that they did not occur.

But again, looking at Scripture from another point of view, and still external to experiment, there is sufficient to warrant such a belief of its Divine origin as to warrant our going on to the experiment of its *power*— and sufficient to outweigh the objections 'lying on the surface' by probabilities on the other hand equally strong. One of the strongest of these, we think, is not only that it is an adaptation to an end which it accomplishes, but an explanation to us of the spiritual mysteries with which we find ourselves surrounded, and which are not elsewhere attempted to be explained — our own spiritual condition, and that in which we find all humanity; the apparent confusion and purposelessness in which the moral world around us seems to be. Scripture purposes to give some explanation, and to be a means of cure for this. It claims a Divine origin in this connection, and when we find so much hitherto and otherwise insoluble here solved, or soluble, it is difficult to deny it the credit which it claims. In this respect it stands in quite another category from any other human possession; and it has not only a key to the spiritual reason and conscience elsewhere unknown, but it speaks to these with authority—with an authority which not only infers connection, but a common origin; a giver and a gift,—that He who speaks is the author of that spoken.

The existence and meaning of Holy Scripture on any other supposition than that of its having a Revelation from God—a Revelation of Himself, and of what we are, and that we may be elevated and benefitted thereby— is more difficult to explain than to take it to be what it claims for itself. On this aspect of Revelation we cannot, I believe, use fewer or better words than those of the apostolic Mr. Erskine, contained in the following words:—'This is the 8th day of the month,' he says, 'and I have been reading the Psalms and Lessons for the day, and I find in all these portions of Scripture, so widely separated from each other in point of time, and in the circumstance of the writers, the breathing of a Holy Spirit revealing to man, as no other voice ever did, his true condition before God, and drawing him up out of that horrible pit into an apprehension of his Heavenly Father's unchangeable purpose of Holy love towards Him, and helping him to rise into fellowship with the Heart, where that purpose ever lives as an everlasting ground of hope and consolation. I feel, after reading these words, as every one must feel who has read the Bible with real earnestness, that there can be no doubt about its origin. And I also feel that its chief object is to help men to know God, and to know themselves in His light, and so be led to receive His Spirit and to become temples of the Holy Ghost. I find with these objects, and coming as it has come to man, it can have but the same origin as man himself— God. Moreover, I feel that a miraculous previous history, such as that of the Jews, according to the Old Testament record, is required as the preparation for the appearance of Jesus Christ. It is required also as the explanation of the difference between the religious knowledge of the Jews and that of all other nations. Does not a miraculous dispensation seem the reasonable and necessary concomitant of that wonderful light shining in the midst of gross darkness, condemning the darkness, and itself condemned by it? God thus taught the people that they were not to be the slaves of matter, but to be free children of Him who governs all things. The miracles of the Bible are not marvels, but illustrations of the character of God, and prophecy is the continual witnessing that in God alone is the redemption of man, and that that redemption is to be accomplished by the way of sorrow and suffering and death.'

But we must pass to some of the specific objections made to Revelation. It is recognised that Scripture, to be what it is claimed to be, must be the gift of God, and if intended to reveal and lead to Him, must be inspired by Him and infallible. 'Now, such inspiration and infallibility,' it is urged, 'must be absolute, if Scripture be what it is claimed to be—the work of God.' 'But,' say they who object to it, 'on the surface we find this contradicted by statements contrary to our experience, and as we think, contrary to truth, so that we cannot accept its origin to be that which it is claimed to be, or bow to its authority.'

Now, to some extent, there is foundation for this exception. It is God's word, we are sure, but we are free to admit that we have the treasure in earthern vessels.

There is, we admit, something of human admixture with the Divine gift; it is not free from human interpolations; it has within it that which, in its first aspect, seems contrary to the order of things or to our experience of them. And further, there is that in it which we cannot suppose to be the addition of human frailty, but to exist in the original constitution of the gift itself, which yet is not in accordance with what we should have expected from a Divine origin.

But while admitting these things, ere passing on to the consideration of them, let us consider first briefly what the meaning of inspiration or infallible guidance, in relation to man, must be. The questions are new, and to some extent have to be treated from the foundation, and we may not find their final solutions for years to come; something, however, may be contributed to their settlement.

The first idea of inspiration and infallible guidance, no doubt, is that which we may call the child-like idea that every word of Scripture is dictated by God, and that the guidance cannot be mistaken or resisted.

A little reflection however will show that this cannot be the true definition.

In the changing and progressive conditions of humanity, with the different degrees of capacity and circumstances men possess, a Revelation such as this must be valueless. Perhaps it might not be impossible to clothe absolute truth such as it appears to the Divine Mind in human language, but it is fair to suppose, that if a Revelation of Divine things is to be made to humanity, it must accept the conditions of humanity and conform to them. It must have reference to time, to circumstances, to individual differences, to imperfection. Revelation is given to raise imperfection to perfection, but it must submit itself to the conditions required. Itself perfect, it must deal with imperfection and accept the necessary conditions. Itself perfect, it is but relatively perfect; absolute perfection would be valueless, as we have seen.

It is perfect, but perfect for a purpose : inspired and infallible, but only so far inspired and infallible as is necessary to effect its purpose. Not indeed in regard to absolute truth (in dealing with that it is absolutely perfect), but in so far as it has need to submit itself to the conditions of means and of degree. Thus, for example in the Old Testament, we see it take up the narratives and beliefs of the day, that thereby it might give a more distinct and definite teaching to the people ; thus it teaches here by a precept, there by a parable as they were able to bear it. And it retains these vestures, as the best mode of conveying Revelation throughout the varying conditions of humanity. Thus it preserves itself, and conveys the lessons to various generations, even as we see the living creatures in our streams make to themselves of straws and pebbles places of habitation and defence for their lives.

It is an instrument adapted to a purpose formed to effect that purpose. Its condition is relative to the purpose : not, as we have said, made so by violation of truth, but by putting itself in the position of those to be taught. And the perception of many truths is but by degree. This is plain in external things; it is equally true, though not so plain, in eternal things. Our first notion, for example, of the sun is that he goes round the earth; when we are in a railway carriage, that the walls and trees rush by us; in learning, that the alphabet, grammars and dictionaries, are the end of the matter. It is so in the same way with spiritual truth, and must be with the Revelation of it. In many cases it must be a thing of time and degree, and the means different from that which we should expect. Revelation has reference to the conditions of humanity, to the end in view, to differences of capacity. It guides to something beyond its words, and often to ends different from the different meaning. As a whole depends on its parts, so the whole of Scripture depends on its parts, but the whole is greater than the parts, and often in its meaning different from and greater than the parts. This is not to be understood to have reference to the real or literal truthfulness of the parts, but the value of the parts, as depending on their being portions of a whole. As portions needful to the whole, they are of the same value as the whole, and invaluable, but as parts away from the whole, they have a value which may be much less.

Revelation rightly taken must be taken as a whole: a whole having an end to accomplish, which it is overruled by God to accomplish, and which it does accomplish; but it is only so far overruled as is needful to accomplish its object. Less than this it is not, and more is not claimed as needful for it. It is an instrument for the accomplishment of an object, divinely fitted to accomplish its object; but it is itself neither the object nor the superintendent; it is different from and other than both, but needful for both and sufficient for their purpose. The question therefore of the Inspiration and Infallible guidance of Scripture is not one of extent but of object; and the question really whether for its purpose the same method is to be pursued, as in all similar cases where knowledge is the medium, namely adaptation and degree, or whether any other method is preferable or possible. If we decide in favour of the former, as in all likelihood we shall, then the only remaining question is, whether Holy Scripture fulfils the conditions which are required?

We believe it does. And this in so peculiar and remarkable a manner, that this itself adds a high probability to its Divine Origin. Whether we consider the varied conditions of humanity, the intellect of the wise and holy, of the savage, of the child, the difference of nations and of individuals, we find provision supplied in Scripture for all: provision suited to their several needs, which they cannot exhaust, and without which we believe the true progress of humanity would be impossible. In this sense the Inspiration and Infallible guidance of Revelation are plenary: plenary for the end in view, and perfect as suited to portions of the way. This is no derogation to Holy Scripture, but a necessity and a merit, since without this adaptation, as we have seen, it would be of little value. If life is an education, our guide must take such steps as those he leads are able to follow, steps which are suitable to their stature, not final steps but progressive towards the end. The end is God, and this is perfectly given in the face of Jesus Christ, the absolute Good and True, but the fulness of the apprehension is by degree, and ~~is not ours, b~~ut as we follow on to know the Lord the Way, the Truth, and Life.

This aspect of Inspiration and of infallible guidance, must not be confounded with that 'doing evil that good may come,' of which the Apostle speaks. It is no making of the end to sanctify the means, but is an adaptation of a higher spiritual to a lower spiritual nature, that the lower may be raised to the higher, by teaching as it is able to bear it, in such methods in short as would be taken in other cases; and it explains the conditions under which we find ourselves and which we find in Revelation. Its basis is not sacrifice of truth, but adaptation to the aspects of humanity, and of the rule, that that which is of value must be sought to be found, a rule eminently true of spiritual things. It is, as it were, a rule, that the Inspiration of Holy Scripture does not lie on the surface; that it does not approve or manifest itself, without seeking. This is eminently characteristic of Holy Scripture, as it is also of the teaching of our Blessed Lord, whose constant warning was, 'He that hath ears to hear,' 'Strive to enter in,' 'The kingdom of Heaven suffereth violence,' and similar expressions. The way of difficulty is ever a condition of receipt. It is a rule at least to a certain point; until, that is, reality is present, and earnestness is felt, and search is true: then the rule changes and it is no more a hidden but an open secret; then an entrance is given to the spiritual kingdom, and Stephen stoned sees 'Heaven opened and Jesus standing at the right hand of God.' But until the first stage is passed the spiritual truths of Scripture are not apprehended although clearly seen by those who have entered in. To them Inspiration and Infallible guidance are no longer a problem, but an experience. It is with this as with all other spiritual things, first that which is natural; then that which is spiritual. Holy Scripture (in its Inspiration and Infallibility), as has been well remarked by an able writer (Dr. Hannah), is like the twofold nature of Our Lord in His humanity and divinity. It is under the conditions of both, and is best understood by considering them together. The human under the conditions of humanity and the divine shining through with a lustre not to be mistaken. The conditions of the one nature give us to a great degree the key to the other.

We cannot well discriminate where the one element begins, and the other ends, the divine and the human; both are there, and there together, separate yet one. It is best to receive them as we find them, neither seeking to divide the natures nor confusing them together; recognising their distinction easily in their extremes on either hand, but not seeking to separate where they join together. They were joined together for our salvation, the voice of God in the words of man: heavenly treasure in earthen vessels.

It will not be necessary here (in the difficulties attending the reception of Holy Scripture) to endeavour to discriminate the different elements which enter into the composition of the sacred canon, the supernatural facts which are strictly so, those deemed so, and those which are but extraordinary manifestations of nature, or extraneous additions, which are but the product of human frailty. At present it is better to leave these to the disentanglation which time and light themselves will make; we must not by curious enquiry be diverted from receiving the purpose of Revelation in the discrimination of puzzling questions. With a few words more, on one topic only, connected with this subject we shall pass to the consideration of other matters. This is the supernatural element existing throughout Scripture, when considered as an objection to its Divine origin.

The existence of this element, we may briefly say, has not been considered by many (and these not the least advanced minds) as being any disparagement to the heavenly origin of Scripture; on the contrary, it is to such rather a recommendation and proof of it. They (and we think rightly) are of opinion, that the attendance of a supernatural outward manifestation was to be expected, and is of the nature of probability rather than otherwise, as consistent with the marvellous and singular outpouring of spiritual gifts and insight, which was possessed, by the exceptional race and position, of the Children of Abraham.

For we must consider that what is called 'miraculous instruction' in any case, is at most but a change in the order of nature (as we know it); we can hardly feel therefore that the presence of such an element in Scripture is any argument against its authenticity. For the ' order of nature' cannot be more than the expression of the will of God, who is not a law but a Living Personality; and whose acting, although according to our experiences, uniform or by law, yet (as nature herself shows us, in the authentic words of her own formation) varies at His will, when there is sufficient reason, of the sufficiency of which He alone is Judge.

To make law so invariable, as some would make it, is to place law in the room of God. But what law is, and what He is, we can easily see, if (for example to discover this) we were to venture to imagine that He should cease to be; then at once we see that law could not stand, but must fall into nothingness as being but the expression of His will alone.

But into these questions we need not further go; nay, we should not so far venture but for their connection with that aspect of Scripture which (being supernatural) takes us beyond the footsteps of humanity. Reverently discussed, we believe that few questions arising out of revelation are fraught with injury:

yea, the existence of a Revelation is a recognition of the fact that knowledge is necessary, and ought to be sought for and possessed by us,—the knowledge of spiritual things.

To return, however, and to close the consideration of the subject of Inspiration, we would briefly sum up its proof and press it upon all as the only sufficient one, viz., an apprehension and experience of its contents. This is the best and perhaps only sufficient proof of its Divine origin as it is assuredly that alone which gives us its benefit. With it our position is beyond controversy, we take the position of the blind man in the gospels, saying, whether it be inspired I know not, one thing I know that whereas I was blind now I see. An empirical perhaps, but a sure position.

The question of the extent of the inspiration of Holy Scripture, I need not inform you, was one of those lately brought for decision to the Court of Privy Council, and was, with those others similarly submitted, left undecided or undefined by it. Considering the position of that Court, as giving, at the most, but the exposition of one particular branch of the Church at large, this was all that it could have done. But its refusal has been objected to as disparagement of the value of dogma, or, as if, on the points submitted, nothing was certainly known, or needful to be believed. But this, if we rightly apprehend the meaning of that Court, was far from being its intention ; as assuredly it is far from being the meaning of those many members of the Church of England, who rejoice at the course which the Court adopted. We believe that the meaning of the Court was (as no doubt it is of those members alluded to), not that dogma should be undervalued, or that there is nothing certainly known, or needful to be believed on the points in question; but that a definition in the direction prayed for, would have been the laying down of false dogma and have been inimical to truth. No mistake can be greater, we believe, than to suppose that the rejoicing at the absence of decision by the Court, was on the ground of its being a disparagement of dogma, or from the belief of the non-necessity of dogma, or its existence on the points in question; the rejoicing was, because the Court did not lay down anything injurious to what was known and believed on the other hand.

Those who were thankful that the Court laid down no definitions in the directions prayed for, had convictions of truth in a direction opposite to the prayers of the petitioners, and believed that the result of decisions in that direction would have effects injurious to truth, and, speaking generally, would have the same effects as have followed similar decisions in other countries; namely, that the letter would supersede the spirit of religion, and Revelation be reduced to a series of formulæ destructive of spiritual life, that religion would be severed from knowledge, and (as is experienced in all such cases) finally severed from morality. This was the cause of their rejoicing. From this great peril, both truth and the Church of England, it is believed, have been alike delivered, and religion, intellect, and morality may still go hand in hand. Had decisions been given in a contrary direction, it is conceived that the Church of England, either like an over nailed tree would have withered on its supports; or eventually have gone down rotting at her anchors; or been left high and dry like those other churches which have taken this course, and are stranded over Christendom. The abstinence of the Court has saved this peril, and its attitude has allowed to the clergy of the Church of England a liberty of prophecy which is to them, it is felt, as an ecclesiastical habeas corpus; even as they had before, in the declaration that 'Holy Scripture containeth all things necessary to Salvaton,' a Magna charta.

Pushed as these decisions would have been to an extreme, the doctrines subjected to them must have hardened into a mould, destructive of both their meaning and their life. The first,—Regeneration in Baptism, could not have escaped being reduced to the condition of a mysterious charm; the second,—the substitution in the Atonement, if necessary to be understood, to a transaction destructive of morality, or if not necessary to be understood, thus rendering a Revelation unnecessary. The Inspiration of Holy Scripture must have been so held as to convert the human intellect into an organic medium, requiring results also in Holy Scripture which in point of fact it does not fulfil; and the last,—the doctrine of Eternal Punishment, must have been converted into a dogma which would have been virtually destructive of the power and unity of God. We doubt not but that the decisions prayed for would have had these or similar effects (on the doctrines submitted to them) and must have made these conclusions the doctrines of the Establisment, and in so doing have severed the nation from the Establishment.

On the first we cannot suppose that a decision given in accordance with Roman Theology would have had any different effect from that which it has in Roman Catholic countries. When we see what the Sacraments are there, we see what that is; that they swallow up and stand in the place of knowledge,—of the knowledge of God, given to us in Revelation; that they are substituted for it, and prevent the new life which flows from Revelation. Making privilege the purport of Revelation, and separating Religion from knowledge, they separate it (as experience shows us to be the invariable consequence) at the same time from morality.

The decision prayed for, in regard to Regeneration by Baptism, is in accordance with an opinion derived from the consequences, supposed inevitable from the bestowal of the rite of Baptism upon infants. Had a decision, however, been given in accordance with that conclusion, it is more probable that the practice of infant Baptism would have been shaken than that such a conclusion as to the meaning of Baptism would have been established. For the Baptism of infants, although sanctioned by pious use and custom, is not so strongly grounded in Scripture as to be able to upset the whole analogy of the faith therein contained. Such faith would not have been overthrown to establish a doctrine, founded alone on a logical deduction from a practice, which, however excellent, has no greater warrant than that derived from custom and propriety. The analogy of faith ever couples spiritual benefit with spiritual knowledge, indeed there is no entrance to the Spirit save through an avenue of its own nature, that is, such as knowledge or belief; and it is impossible that this rule and analogy (which are the foundations of Revelation) could either admit of, or be consistent with, the admission of a principle, which is destructive of it.

The tendency of the decision prayed for, the reception of spiritual benefit by material instrumentality (ex opere operato), would undoubtedly have had this effect, and should not therefore have been sought for by any not desirous of this result. It is probable that those who pressed for such decision did not desire, and were not aware, that such would be the conclusion.

And indeed such a view of Baptism would place the justice of the Universal Father in a false position; making his blessings appertain arbitrarily to persons, and not to be conditions consequent on conduct. Assuredly the Saviour of mankind took the little children, and laid His hands upon them and blessed them, not because they were Jews, but because they were little children. The benefit to the Jew was not a personal one (although his selfishness would have made it so), but a relative one, because he possessed the ' oracles ' that is, the knowledge of God. 'Salvation is of the Jews' it is written, and this because they knew what they worshipped; salvation being consequent on knowledge, as all spiritual benefit must be. In Scripture, eternal life is described as the result of 'knowing God' and acquiring a conformity to Him, the result of knowledge. The command, therefore to baptise all nations, was a command to enlighten all nations, to enlighten them with the knowledge of God; to make God known to men, that men might be saved by that knowledge. It was to be a knowledge contained in the Name into which they were to be baptised—the name of 'Father, Son and Holy Ghost.' The Apostles were to make known unto men therefore that there is an Almighty Father, that is, that God is a Father, and Almighty; that there is a Divine Son, in and with whom they are sons; and an Holy Spirit into which they are to be born as new creatures. It was a Revelation, they were to make unto the nations, whereby they were to be brought nigh to God. A baptism into knowledge, into the knowledge of God. Had it been otherwise no knowledge would have been required, and a Revelation would have been unnecessary. As it was not so, and a Revelation was given, we must conclude that knowledge is necessary, and that a Baptism irrespective of it, is in its consequences profitless, yea more, for we know that where the offices of religion are performed irrespective of knowledge, religion severed from knowledge ceases to be the efficient of morality, becomes separated from it, and indeed in time comes to take the place of it, than which there can be no greater perversion. When Baptism becomes reduced to a rite, and its recipients are not distinguishable from the unjust extortioners and adulterers of this world, we must conclude that Baptism apart from knowledge is apart from blessing; that where there is no blessing there is no Baptism rightly understood; that Baptism which is not the efficient of holiness is no true Baptism, and that holiness is alone possible through knowledge and belief. We are not the children of God because we are baptised, we are baptised because we are His children, and they only who are led by His Spirit are His sons. That Spirit leadeth all, and they may follow if they will. Let us not bind God's Holy Spirit, especially in any wise which disconnects It from the gifts of Christ or makes It not co-equal with the gift, which is co-equal in extent with humanity.

The condition of the question of substitution in the Atonement is somewhat akin to that of Regeneration in Baptism.

It has derived its aspect (of virtue irrespective of knowledge) from the same cause as Baptism; a non-recognition, that is, of the truth that spiritual benefit is contingent on spiritual enlightenment. The idea of the

Atonement which is represented by substitution, has no doubt been much furthered by its connection with that view of Sacrifice in the Roman mass, of which the basis is substitution; and it has also been taken up and fostered in another way by the Reformation; which desiring to make an end of human merit, and its transference in the saints, retained the idea without the perception of its intrinsic erroneousness, thinking it fit and safe if associated alone with Christ.

The conception of the work of the Redeemer in His descent to seek and to save those who were lost, as being a transaction of merit capable of negotiable transference, is so marvellous a mistake that it would scarce be credible, had it not so extensively prevailed, and did it not even now go far to colour a great region of theology. Yet, strangely, those who hold this doctrine as right in ecclesiastical, would not admit it in civil transactions. It is a doctrine which those who hold are no doubt unaware that virtually it severs the unity of the Deity. In taking a transaction between two persons which infers their diversity, and setting the attributes of God in antagonism to one another, it is a doctrine contrary to the nature of things, and to the analogy of faith, and is only capable of discovery or defence by detaching a portion of Revelation from its context and giving it a meaning of its own, or by exalting the letter over the spirit of Scripture, and putting authority in the place of reason.

No doubt there are expressions in Holy Scripture which may be held to favour it, and also in our formularies, more especially in that for the Holy Communion. Yet it is impossible that substitution literally understood can be their real meaning, seeing that it lowers the work and person of the Saviour, yea, and the character of

Almighty God. Whatever the truth may be, it cannot be that the Atonement is of the nature of a negociable equivalent. Let us consider the history of the Atonement, and attempt to discern that in it from which this idea took its rise. The Atonement was a work of grace, the grace of our Lord Jesus Christ for humanity. Unable to help themselves, tied and bound in ignorance and in sin, the Lord descended for men's salvation—unable to force their way through the dark valley He broke a passage for them—unable to find God, He led them to the Father. Indifferent or opposed as they were to Him, He bore the burden alone. He poured out His life in their service. By death He opened to them light and life—light and the eternal life, which comes by knowing the Father in the Son. By His poverty He made them rich; by His stripes He healed, and still heals, by showing them the nature of sin and the nature of God, drawing them out of themselves to God and goodness. This is the grace of Christ, and the shape in which it appeared. It was an Atonement, a bringing nigh of God and man, a deliverance, a redemption, a restoration of man. It is a work having for its object the conformity of the human nature to the Divine. An Atonement or making as one two different natures—a means of giving to the human nature the character of the Divine. It is the way whereby man is brought out of sin into righteousness. No substitution could do this. No one becoming righteous in place of another can effect for the other that which it is necessary that he himself should be—it would indeed prevent instead of effecting it. Sacrifice in place of obedience in this sense is inadmissible, for a substitutionary sacrifice would frustrate the end in view. Salvation is a healing of the soul, a rectification or making righteous of it; a deliverance from sin, not from penalty; from disease, not from its remedy. It contains, indeed, a pardon; but not one which clears the guilty by removing penalty. It does not do this, for death still reigns. It does remove penalty, but by lifting into righteousness and out of the reach of penalty thereby, not by interfering with the legal sanction. It is a work, and Christ's work, and that for others; but not that there should be no more work or that they should not work, but that there might be, and that they might do it. Without Him it could not be done. But He acted and suffered that we might do so, giving us a motive, showing us the way, leaving us an example to walk in his steps—that bearing in our bodies the dying of the Lord Jesus, and saying with Him, 'Lo! I come to do Thy will, O God,' sin might be destroyed and an everlasting righteousness be brought in. It is manifest that substitution would not effect this; that another, being what we ought to be, could not in this respect benefit us; that righteousness being the end of the matter, and a personal fitness and holiness, the condition of Heaven, and the only thing which is or can give blessedness; a salvation which is not based upon this must be a delusion. Substitution, in this sense, therefore, cannot be the meaning of the Atonement, but must be some misapprehension or perversion of the true meaning. It is probable that this has arisen out of that strange and unhappy condition of our nature, which realises more readily and more profoundly the magisterial than the Fatherly aspect of our God, a condition which we find even the more general and profound, as humanity sinks in the scale of intelligence. It has, no doubt, also its counterpart among the intelligent, when the error is committed of associating weakness with the Fatherly aspect—a great misapprehension. Based, as the Fatherly character is, on the attribute of love, it is supposed that this will lead, if it stands alone, to weakness or imperfection in justice. The very reverse is the case, if it be rightly understood what love is—love is amiable, and the paternal aspect as based on it is amiable also, but there is no attribute so stern or rigid as love in the enforcement of righteousness, and this is because it knows there is no other way to blessedness, and love enforces righteousness therefore beyond what is required by any other ruling power. We shall understand this most fully if we realise the acting of the paternal character, or love as opposed to mere fulfilment in ourselves. Let any one who is a father imagine his son falling into vice and being tried by a magistrate,—would it satisfy him if his son were, by an arbitrary exercise of the magistrate's authority, to be, as it is called, 'let off?' Would this satisfy a father—would anything satisfy him short of the restoration to righteousness of his son? A magistrate may be lenient, he may perhaps be able to accept of compensation, but a father can be satisfied with nothing but righteousness, as love knows that no other thing is good. The paternal is higher than the magisterial capacity, even among us. Must it not also be so in the highest regions? Surely it is a proof of our debasement, to lower the Divine Standard below the human. No doctrine can be true which is founded on such a basis, and if on a different basis from the human, the Divine cannot be on a lower but on a higher platform of morality, and can only be at any time imagined to be so, for some false conception of premises which result in so false a conclusion. The Atonement can have no real resemblance to a negotiable equivalent. As we increase in the knowledge of God, we rise in our conceptions of the Divine morality, as we apprehend Christ Jesus we apprehend more clearly the nature of His sacrifice, that He lived and died for us that we might not live and die unto ourselves,—that He was righteousness for us that we might be righteous,—that He lived and died for us, leaving an example that we should follow in His steps, opening up to us the way to God, showing us the Father, weaning us from sin, making us new creatures, giving us a nature which cannot be ours by being His,—but being His, was His that it might be ours; it being His for us, not instead of being ours, but that it might be ours, and so gave it, living and dying for us as (although of His own nature infinitely higher) a mother dies in giving birth to her children, a patriot in giving liberty to his country, a martyr in establishing his faith.

The doctrine of substitution if held in its entire nakedness cannot but lead to one of two conclusions,—to immorality or to infidelity; the former of which is too often exhibited in Roman Catholic countries where absolution waits on substitution; and the latter, in Calvinistic countries, where the Divine government is believed to be so conducted, as to be exercised in an exceptional way on a limited number.

But the whole question of the meaning of the Atonement is often shelved by the apparently pious declaration that 'into the meaning of such divine mysteries (as it is expressed) we must not narrowly enquire, for they are in their essence probably beyond us.' And in some sort this is true. But it is also true, that they must have some meaning, and that it was intended that we should know this meaning, else would there have been no Revelation, or they no part of it; and even more, that without this increasing knowledge being ours, we are not and cannot be benefited by the Atonement, as spiritual benefit can only arise by spiritual enlightenment and improvement.

The question of Inspiration has been already considered and has been seen to be, one rather of purpose for an end, or relative than absolute and general, save in so far as the nature of God Himself is concerned, and truth is not infringed.

The last question, that of Eternal Punishment, is that which presents the greatest difficulty, not from its inherent difficulty but from its involving so many relative consequences. Generally speaking most men are not in a state to consider it with advantage, and it labours also under much misapprehension from confusion of ideas. Treated in the way which leaves the impression that 'it signifies little what men do, seeing that it will be all right in the end,' few doctrines could be more injurious. Considered as affecting the purposes and character of God, and our own connection with these doctrines, few can be more beneficial: much misapprehension exists on the question from confusion of ideas, from mixing up the idea of Immortality with that of Eternal Life.

In Holy Scripture while Immortality is plainly revealed in connection with the Redemption which is in Christ Jesus, the Eternal life which is alluded to generally in connection with it means a different thing, and does not so much relate to exemption from death or to a resurrection from it, as to a character or condition of life and state which is the product of knowledge and unity with God, the nature of which is Eternal. Of this it is, that was said, 'it is Life Eternal to know Thee the only true God,' and, 'he that hath the Son hath Life;' and, 'we have passed from death unto life;' and again (of its converse) 'he that loveth not his brother abideth in death.' It is a kind or character of life that is spoken of, which has the nature of Eternity in it. Whether this be from the constitution of things, or is in connection with the gift of Christ, does not matter.

He that hath this, hath Eternal Life. He that hath not this hath not Eternal Life. He that is not in this life, is not in the Eternal Life spoken of in Scripture. As we lay hold of it, we are in it, as we let it slip we are out of it, as we abide or abide not in it, it is ours or not. It is ours through Christ, as the mind is in us which was in Christ Jesus.

Here the question arises whether it is the will of God that all men should have this life. And this is answered by determining the extent of the gift of Christ: and of this it is written that 'He tasted death for every man,' and that He is the seed in whom all the families of the Earth are to be blessed. The gift of Christ is to every man therefore, and the grace of the Eternal Life must be coequal with it. The conclusion then arrives—at what time and how is this end to be accomplished? Is the purpose and process connected with this life only, or does it extend beyond it? If to this life only, then the will of God is not accomplished, for of the multitudes who die here it is evident that few are partakers of this life. Is it therefore continued beyond this life? Is the process continuous until its end is accomplished? What is the nature of our relation to God? If that of children to a parent, is it limited to this life? Does it cease with the grave and then a new relationship begin? What is the character of the Divine Government? Is

F

punishment corrective or vindictive? Does Eternal Punishment mean an Eternal antagonism to sin taking the form of penalty while sin lasts, that thereby sin may be destroyed; or is it an infinite antagonism to sin taking the form of vindictiveness without end? Is the law of 'overcoming evil with good' an universal law of God's kingdom, and punishment a form of it? or what is the law?

These and similar questions have to be dealt with ere we can come to a decision on this question.

We may sum it up as follows. The gift of Life which is in Christ Jesus is limited to those who are in Christ Jesus. He is however the Saviour of all men, and this is a literal truth; at what time is this salvation to be accomplished?

Looking at the question apart from Scripture it is plain that 'evil having nothing Divine in it, is essentially finite, not infinite' (Gurney) and must have an end: and that to deny this is nothing less, than to set up what Theologians would call Manicheeism, or the being of two Gods.

But the question must be tried at the bar of Scripture; for there alone can it be settled; as there alone have we any Revelation of it.

What then saith the Scripture? It is notorious that there are express terms wherein the doctrine of Eternal Punishment is laid down; and that some of the strongest of these are in the words of the Lord Himself. And further that it would be trifling with these words to attach any than their natural meaning to them. But on the other hand it is true that there are expressions equally strong the other way; that for instance the scope of the argument of the great Epistle to the Gentiles is summed up in favour of the final restitution of all things with the words, 'I beseech you therefore by the mercies of God,' and again, that the conclusion of Revelation is, 'that every creature which is in Heaven and on the Earth, and under the Earth, and such as are in the Sea,' shall rejoice.

The demand therefore in fine is, what is the ruling aspect of Scripture, and how is it ascertained? Are the words of our Lord as to Eternal Punishment to be taken literally, or to be taken as in other places (such as those alluding to the destruction of Jerusalem), with an explanatory comment? Or are we to ascertain the meaning by the sense in which the Church has taken it? The mediæval Church, for example, if the words be taken literally, teaches that the Holy Spirit operates for Salvation beyond the grave. But on this ground as to doctrine, too much weight must never be laid, for the failure and extinction of the Church in so many places, show that some defects must have existed, and probably still exist, of which it is fair to say that erroneous doctrine on this point may be one cause. The general analogy of the faith and that which we know to be the Divine nature can alone guide us safely. Limiting however the question to the recent action of the Church of England, it is plain that she ought not to do other than she has done lately, when it is remembered that she teaches as one of her fundamental doctrines that the Redemption which is in Christ Jesus is universal, or that Christ is the Redeemer of all men; putting into the mouths of all her little ones the touching words 'Who hath redeemed me and all mankind.'

It is impossible that she could recede from or deny this declaration, or so trifle with it by definition as to annul or impair it. This confession is her glory among the churches which have shared in the Reformation; and it is her strength; and that which probably attracts and attaches the most devoted and intelligent of her children.

It would not be expedient perhaps to extend this confession into details, compromising questions of mode and time; but she could not withdraw from what she has said, but for the truth's sake. She has not done so, and we trust never will. If she does, she may then write Ichabod over all her greatness.

But I must conclude. I have considered with you the bearings of the late decisions of the Church of England, and found them to be good. Not so much indeed from anything which they contain, as from their being a protest against that conventional religion which rests on authority, and has no corresponding response within the heart: and also from their being a barrier against that fixing of truth in new formulas which would deprive it of life, and hinder its reflection of additional brightness.

In the examination of the connection of authority with truth however, it must not be supposed that there is any desire to set aside or undervalue authority itself; all that is desired or was attempted has been to ascertain and to put it into its proper place. This we have considered to be ancillary or relative;—that authority is no integral part or necessity of truth. It is needful; but only as introductory, it is not so beyond this. We must commence with authority. A child for example is taught that two and two make four, but after it has heard this it must go on to learn that two and two *do* make four: that is, it must go on to the reason of the thing; and to understand and to receive it in its own proper light. It is also thus in Revelation, and we must go on from obedience on authority, to understanding and to sympathise with the things revealed. It cannot be said that we have received or are possessed of Revelation in any true sense before we do this.

The extreme form of that religion which rests its conclusions on authority, is only to be found fully exemplified in the Church of Rome; it exists however in embryo among ourselves, and may be developed more largely at any time by circumstances, as indeed it has been already in these later years.

As being destructive (if logically followed out) of entrance into the kingdom of the truth by experience of it, it cannot be too closely watched, or protested against; and even when held but implicitly, its premises cannot but be fraught with the greatest peril. We see the character of principles by their results; and if a result is manifestly inconsistent with the original purpose of a thing, we may be sure that the principle which leads to this result is erroneous. If the highest form of a religion which rests everything on authority, is that with which we are conversant in recluses, such as monks and nuns, which indeed it is; then the ideal of mankind is so different from that which undoubtedly was the ideal of mankind in the mind of the Creator, that the principles which lead to it cannot be correct. Obedience to authority irrespective of reason, subjection to the Church (as it is called) until the individual becomes dead 'utpote cadaver' (the highest form of such religion);—this is so far removed from the ideal of the use of the powers with which we are gifted by God, that principles which lead to it and its results partake more, we must say, of the nature of sin than of aught other, and as a moral suicide cannot be looked upon as merely erroneous, but as having in it of the nature of guilt, for no abberation of liberty save to the extent of insanity, can be so hopeless as this aberration, since there is no deliverance from a war ending in death.

But putting aside the arguments from results, the question of Revelation (and of all else) is,—whether its truths stand by their intrinsic value or not, whether its light shines by its own light, or by the light of others?—whether the Church is enlightened by the Truth, or the Truth by the Church; whether it is the Truth which makes the Church, or the Church the Truth, whether Revelation comes to the Church or from the Church?

And this, in brief, is indeed the controversy between the Church of England and the Church of Rome, and as the banner of the latter is inscribed with the words of Augustine, 'Evangelis non crederem nisi me cogeret ecclesiæ catholicæ auctoritas,' so is the former with the words of St. Paul, ' But though we or an angel from heaven preach any other gospel unto you than that which we have preached unto you, let him be accursed.' And we doubt not that the victory is with the latter; nay, so confusing have grown the claims which have to be considered ere the true guide is found (for the Roman but contests the place with other churches) that it is more easy to find the end than the guide who should lead to it: God than the human guide who is to conduct to Him.

But God cannot be found in this way. God is not God by human authority, and cannot be found by it. A man cannot worship the God of another man, be He the true God: a man must worship his own God: God must be God to him; he must have a God of his own, and God must be his God. God is not our God either by the verdict of majorities or by signs, but by being born in our hearts. We recognise Him because He has given us power to do so by creating us in His image. We are His children, and He is our Father. To this the Revelation comes, by this it is received, the appeal is made to that which we already have, and which if we had not, the appeal must be fruitless. We are the sons of God! when it pleases Him to reveal the sonship in us, then we know it. The revelation and sonship are from Him. No external power effects this. The Church is not the author or creator of this truth. She is the witness of it only. Revelation comes to the Church not from the Church. The truth of God comes to us by a birth of His own nature within us, our souls being that candle of the Lord which His Spirit lighteneth. His Spirit witnesses with our spirit; and the capacity in us for this shows us, what was meant to be, and which can alone be.

Let us look at this once more.

Salvation cometh by knowledge of the truth, and the truth is received by the spirit. We require truth, we receive it by the spirit. Scripture contains the truth, we apprehend it by the spirit in which it was written; when we have done so we question not its origin nor its authority from the region into which it takes us. It is thus we attain Christianity, to be that which Christ was, to have that which Christ gives: more than this we cannot have, more than this we cannot ask. Theology will not give this; it profits not those who are exercised therein. Carnal self and natural reason enter into theologians and make them use their science, as others use their science and profession for their own ends. Theology will not heal spiritual disorder. It gives not that which is the end of religion, holy love and joy: and if it gives not the end, it is not the way. The end is to be as Christ was, and the way is by sitting at His feet as a little child. This is the only theology which will profit, the only theology which is sound. We would not discourage learning or learned research, more than any other labour, but if we would draw nigh to God and find Him it is not by or in a learned theology. That alone which will bring us near, or find what we seek, is the essential teaching of God Himself;—God by the Spirit illuminating the Word, this is that alone which will give us what we seek and what we need.

It is a kingdom which draweth nigh, which is coming to all men, for all shall thus know the Lord, and need no man to teach them ; it is so in the nature of things, it is so from express promises in Holy Writ, it is so from the nature and character of God. Of its coming we have assurance, it is contained in the character of God. That the future of creation is hopeful is assured from the character of God—as He is, *it* must be. His perfections are the security for its happiness. A righteous Father loveth righteousness, and an Almighty Father doeth what He will. A loving Father does the best thing in his power for his children ; an Almighty Father hath the best thing in His power. That God is this, and that we are His children, that He doeth and will do His best thing, we may not doubt; and therefore it is written, that the time cometh when ' every ' creature which is in Heaven and on the earth and ' under the earth, and such as are in the sea, and all that ' are in them,' are to say, ' Blessing, and honour, and ' glory, and power, be unto Him that sitteth upon the ' throne, and unto the Lamb for ever.' And that which is to be—that best thing for us—is, that we should be as He is; that we should in our measure be partakers of the Divine nature. There is but one blessing for moral beings,—it is in righteousness. This blessing it is which we are to have. There is but one way in which such blessing can come to finite beings —by time, by degree, by education, by experience. That way is ours. God puts His moral offspring in the way whereby they may obtain it. He surrounds them with circumstances of choice. He gives them to choose and to refuse, and He attaches consequences which teach their own lessons. Thus it is that we are as we are. We are chastened that we may be partakers of the Divine Holiness. Life is an education. The end is certain, and so is the way; both are secured and guaranteed by the nature and character of God. We have an infallible guidance to a secured end; assurance and guidance which rest on the infinite love of Jehovah. That is our assurance and our infallibility. There is no other, and we can want no other, inasmuch as these rest on and arise out of the necessities of the Divine nature. An Infinite Love must do the best for every one, and righteousness being that best, it will not cease until its purpose is effected. Nor is our assurance based upon exceptions or condescension (rightly understood), but on the infinite necessities of the Divine nature; that what ought to be must be, yea, and now is. True it is, that he has not this assurance, who knows not what ought to be, or in other words, what love and righteousness are; but he who knows this, knows what ought to be, and what must be, yea, and what in reality now is. God is the best thing in the universe, and that best thing we know to be Love, and we know that the acts of God must be in accordance with His character. The future of creation, therefore, must be as He is, and that is good—not good because of anything in the creature, but good because of that which is in the Creator. He is a Father, and therefore despiseth not, neither forgetteth the work of His own hands. As He creates in love, so He continues in this love the works of His creation, continuing and increasing His gifts for ever. It was from no necessity that He created; from no need of a creation, but from love, which is infinite, from love which, as it was in the beginning, is and ever shall be infinitely the same. This is one ground of assurance for the future well-being of creation, that it will go on to many and ever increasingly joyful mansions. This end is sure, and the way is also sure. The way may be dark, the times and seasons are the secrets of the Lord; a nature has to be produced in us requiring time and pain. There is a night of sorrow ere joy cometh in the morning; ere the son becomes manifestly the Son of God, of a Divine Father. There is friction needed for the diamond, a burial for the seed. We are chastened that we may be made meet; it is one salvation, in the way and the end. Both are sure. It is the redemption which is in Christ Jesus, the restitution of all things. Let us make sure of it, and lay hold of the eternal life. It is not a name, it is a reality; it must be our own not another's. Let us not turn it into a word; let us not fix it into a formula. Sealing the stone and setting a watch upon it will give us but a dead Redeemer, or if in such we look for Him, He will not be there. He will have risen, we shall see but the place where the Lord lay. We must bear Him about in our body, and have in us the mind which was in Christ Jesus; thus shall we pass from imperfection to perfection, from death unto life. But the end is hindered and delayed—hindered by our sins and shortcomings. The perversity of man hinders his own happiness, and the Saints cry, and have cried, 'Lord, how long?' Without us they cannot be perfected, nor the end come. It is a long expectation, and we have to wait, but the end shall come. As yet we see not all things put under the Redeemer; the will of man as contrary to that of God is still done, and it is not on earth as it is in Heaven; but the Kingdom is coming and shall come, and God's will shall be done, and God be all in all. We see not this as yet, but we see Jesus, and in seeing Him we see the earnest and pledge of the good that is to be, of more than we can ask or think. If we who are evil can do good to our children, how much more He—the Perfect Father—the Father of all—the Father everlasting?

One word of explanation, and farewell. If I have said anything which seems to bear hard on those who hold any opinion different from my own, I pray to be forgiven. I would not wound any person of any opinion; it is to the opinions themselves I am opposed, and some of them seem to me so dangerous that I should be wanting in true love to any brother if I did not say of them that which I think. I say it for the good, as I deem it, of my brother. I believe much mischief arises from calling things by their wrong names out of a false charity. Of evils which in the time of the Reformation and of the Scriptures we should have been delivered from, by plain speaking, we are now the victims. Coquetting with practices or opinions alien from our Church or Creed, would have been called of old by names now seldom mentioned even—spiritual adultery or fornication. Who has not seen the mischief to the younger members of families from such coquettings?

The severing of parent and child, at the hearth and at the altar. That which through tenderness and toleration has been winked at, becoming at last so bold as to turn round and accuse the Mother, or, at least, apologise for her—the Mother Church of England, that pure and righteous mother!

I should not be a true governor or shepherd of Israel did I not speak of this, as I feel it, with a righteous indignation.

Looking at these things in their results, and looking at them in the light of eternity, we cannot but call things by their right names, or do other than speak of them with due solemnity. Especially must they do so who hold offices of spiritual responsibility.

But those who know what love is, and what the truth is, and what these things we have spoken of are, will excuse and forgive any freedom which has been taken; they will know that we are not their enemy because we speak the truth, as it appears to us, and they will believe that we speak as we do, from our heart's desire for their edification.

If I have written these pages in the defence of the Church of England, who am among the least worthy 'of all the sons she hath brought up,' it is to be excused by the necessity of the times, and by the silence of those more worthy. It is possible that one now removed from the dust and toil of the warfare may judge more clearly of the war, and that one gifted through the blessing of sickness, with the sight of various forms of Christianity, may be able to contribute some earnest assurance, and to give the verdict of experience, in the opinions which he entertains.

It does not seem to me that the majority of the Clergy and Laity of the Church of England are sufficiently aware of the great treasure which they possess in the extraordinary beauty and feelings of the Church established among them,—that Canaan of Christendom whose fields are so thickly sown with the preparation of the Gospel of peace; nor of the riches of their own 'inviolate island,' where righteousness and truth embrace each other, because the Word of God is by every hearth, and none but Christ is upon the altar. A Church and land which never were so fair as now, that the Word of God is unbound and the Spirit has free course to illuminate and enlarge its letter. May it be our care to preserve this freedom, and to maintain the foundation on which it rests; the foundation and freedom of the Word of God, as delivered once for all unto the saints, and enlightened continuously and increasingly by His Holy Spirit.

39 Paternoster Row, E.C.
London, *July* 1865.

# GENERAL LIST OF WORKS,

## NEW BOOKS AND NEW EDITIONS,
### PUBLISHED BY
### Messrs. LONGMANS, GREEN, READER, and DYER.

---

| | | | |
|---|---|---|---|
| Arts, Manufactures, &c. | 11 | Knowledge for the Young | 20 |
| Astronomy, Meteorology, Popular Geography, &c. | 7 | Miscellaneous and Popular Metaphysical Works | 6 |
| Biography and Memoirs | 3 | Natural History and Popular Science | 8 |
| Chemistry, Medicine, Surgery, and the Allied Sciences | 9 | Periodical Publications | 20 |
| Commerce, Navigation, and Mercantile Affairs | 18 | Poetry and the Drama | 17 |
| Criticism, Philology, &c. | 4 | Religious Works | 12 |
| Fine Arts and Illustrated Editions | 10 | Rural Sports, &c. | 17 |
| General and School Atlases | 19 | Travels, Voyages, &c. | 15 |
| Historical Works | 1 | Works of Fiction | 16 |
| Index | 21—24 | Works of Utility and General Information | 18 |

---

## *Historical Works.*

**The History of England from** the Fall of Wolsey to the Death of Elizabeth. By James Anthony Froude, M.A. late Fellow of Exeter College, Oxford.

Vols. I. to IV. the Reign of Henry VIII. Third Edition, 54s.

Vols. V. and VI. the Reigns of Edward VI. and Mary. Second Edition, 28s.

Vols. VII. and VIII. the Reign of Elizabeth, Vols. I. and II. Third Edition, 28s.

**The History of England from** the Accession of James II. By Lord Macaulay. Three Editions, as follows.

Library Edition, 5 vols. 8vo. £4.
Cabinet Edition, 8 vols. post 8vo. 48s.
People's Edition, 4 vols. crown 8vo. 16s.

**Revolutions in English History.** By Robert Vaughan, D.D. 3 vols. 8vo. 45s.

Vol. I. Revolutions of Race, 15s.
Vol. II. Revolutions in Religion, 15s.
Vol. III. Revolutions in Government, 15s.

**An Essay on the History of the** English Government and Constitution, from the Reign of Henry VII. to the Present Time. By John Earl Russell. Third Edition, revised, with New Introduction. Crown 8vo. 6s.

**The History of England during** the Reign of George the Third. By William Massey, M.P. 4 vols. 8vo. 48s.

**The Constitutional History of** England, since the Accession of George III. 1760—1860. By Thomas Erskine May, C.B. Second Edition. 2 vols. 8vo. 33s.

**Historical Studies.** I. On some of the Precursors of the French Revolution; II. Studies from the History of the Seventeenth Century; III. Leisure Hours of a Tourist. By Herman Merivale, M.A. 8vo. 12s. 6d.

**Lectures on the History of England.** By William Longman. Vol. I. from the Earliest Times to the Death of King Edward II. with 6 Maps, a coloured Plate, and 53 Woodcuts. 8vo. 15s.

**A Chronicle of England,** from B.C. 55 to A.D. 1485; written and illustrated by J. E. DOYLE. With 81 Designs engraved on Wood and printed in Colours by E. Evans. 4to. 42s.

**History of Civilization.** By HENRY THOMAS BUCKLE. 2 vols. £1 17s.

VOL. I. *England and France,* Fourth Edition, 21s.

VOL. II. *Spain and Scotland,* Second Edition, 16s.

**Democracy in America.** By ALEXIS DE TOCQUEVILLE. Translated by HENRY REEVE, with an Introductory Notice by the Translator. 2 vols. 8vo. 21s.

**The Spanish Conquest in** America, and its Relation to the History of Slavery and to the Government of Colonies. By ARTHUR HELPS. 4 vols. 8vo. £3. VOLS. I. & II. 28s. VOLS. III. & IV. 16s. each.

**History of the Reformation in** Europe in the Time of Calvin. By J. H. MERLE D'AUBIGNÉ, D.D. VOLS. I. and II. 8vo. 28s. and VOL. III. 12s.

**Library History of France,** in 5 vols. 8vo. By EYRE EVANS CROWE. VOL. I. 14s. VOL. II. 15s. VOL. III. 18s. VOL. IV. nearly ready.

**Lectures on the History of** France. By the late Sir JAMES STEPHEN, LL.D. 2 vols. 8vo. 24s.

**The History of Greece.** By C. THIRL-WALL, D.D. Lord Bishop of St. David's. 8 vols. 8vo. £3; or in 8 vols. fcp. 28s.

**The Tale of the Great Persian** War, from the Histories of Herodotus. By GEORGE W. COX, M.A. late Scholar of Trin. Coll. Oxon. Fcp. 7s. 6d.

**Ancient History of Egypt, As-** syria, and Babylonia. By the Author of 'Amy Herbert.' Fcp. 8vo. 6s.

**Critical History of the Lan-** guage and Literature of Ancient Greece. By WILLIAM MURE, of Caldwell. 5 vols. 8vo. £3 9s.

**History of the Literature of** Ancient Greece. By Professor K. O. MÜLLER. Translated by the Right Hon. Sir GEORGE CORNEWALL LEWIS, Bart. and by J. W. DONALDSON, D.D. 3 vols. 8vo. 36s.

**History of the Romans under** the Empire. By CHARLES MERIVALE, B.D. Chaplain to the Speaker.

CABINET EDITION, 8 vols. post 8vo. 48s.

LIBRARY EDITION, 7 vols. 8vo. £5. 11s.

**The Fall of the Roman Re-** public: a Short History of the Last Century of the Commonwealth. By the same Author. 12mo. 7s. 6d.

**The Conversion of the Roman** Empire: the Boyle Lectures for the year 1864, delivered at the Chapel Royal, Whitehall. By the same. 2nd Edition. 8vo. 8s. 6d.

**Critical and Historical Essays** contributed to the *Edinburgh Review.* By the Right Hon. Lord MACAULAY.

LIBRARY EDITION, 3 vols. 8vo. 36s.

TRAVELLER'S EDITION, in 1 vol. 21s.

In POCKET VOLUMES, 3 vols. fcp. 21s.

PEOPLE'S EDITION, 2 vols. crown 8vo. 8s.

**Historical and Philosophical** Essays. By NASSAU W. SENIOR. 2 vols. post 8vo. 16s.

**History of the Rise and Influence** of the Spirit of Rationalism in Europe. By W. E. H. LECKY, M.A. Second Edition. 2 vols. 8vo. 25s.

**The Biographical History of** Philosophy, from its Origin in Greece to the Present Day. By GEORGE HENRY LEWES. Revised and enlarged Edition. 8vo. 16s.

**History of the Inductive Sciences.** By WILLIAM WHEWELL, D.D. F.R.S. Master of Trin. Coll. Cantab. Third Edition. 3 vols. crown 8vo. 24s.

**Egypt's Place in Universal His-** tory; an Historical Investigation. By C. C. J. BUNSEN, D.D. Translated by C. H. COTTRELL, M.A. With many Illustrations. 4 vols. 8vo. £5 8s. VOL. V. is nearly ready, completing the work.

**Maunder's Historical Treasury;** comprising a General Introductory Outline of Universal History, and a Series of Separate Histories. Fcp. 10s.

**Historical and Chronological En-** cyclopædia, presenting in a brief and convenient form Chronological Notices of all the Great Events of Universal History. By B. B. WOODWARD, F.S.A. Librarian to the Queen. [*In the press.*

**History of the Christian Church,** from the Ascension of Christ to the Conversion of Constantine. By E. BURTON, D.D. late Regius Prof. of Divinity in the University of Oxford. Eighth Edition. Fcp. 3s. 6d.

**Sketch of the History of the** Church of England to the Revolution of 1688. By the Right Rev. T. V. SHORT, D.D. Lord Bishop of St. Asaph. Sixth Edition. Crown 8vo. 10s. 6d.

**History of the Early Church,** from the First Preaching of the Gospel to the Council of Nicæa, A.D. 325. By the Author of 'Amy Herbert.' Fcp. 4s. 6d.

**The English Reformation.** By F. C. MASSINGBERD, M.A. Chancellor of Lincoln and Rector of South Ormsby. Third Edition, revised and enlarged. Fcp. 6s.

**History of Wesleyan Methodism.** By GEORGE SMITH, F.A.S Fourth Edition, with numerous Portraits. 3 vols, crown 8vo. 7s. each.

**Villari's History of Savonarola** and of his Times, translated from the Italian by LEONARD HORNER, F.R.S. with the co-operation of the Author. 2 vols. post 8vo. with Medallion, 18s.

**Lectures on the History of Modern** Music, delivered at the Royal Institution. By JOHN HULLAH, Professor of Vocal Music in King's College and in Queen's College, London. FIRST COURSE, with Chronological Tables, post 8vo. 6s. 6d. SECOND COURSE, on the Transition Period, with 26 Specimens, 8vo. 16s.

## *Biography and Memoirs.*

**Letters and Life of Francis** Bacon, including all his Occasional Works. Collected and edited, with a Commentary, by J. SPEDDING, Trin. Coll. Cantab. VOLS. I. and II. 8vo. 24s.

**Passages from the Life of a Philosopher.** By CHARLES BABBAGE, Esq. M.A. F.R.S. &c. 8vo. 12s.

**Life of Robert Stephenson, F.R.S.** By J. C. JEAFFRESON, Barrister-at-Law, and WILLIAM POLE, F.R.S. Memb. Inst. Civ. Eng. With 2 Portraits and 17 Illustrations. 2 vols. 8vo. 32s.

**Life of the Duke of Wellington.** By the Rev. G. R. GLEIG, M.A. Popular Edition, carefully revised; with copious Additions. Crown 8vo. with Portrait, 5s.

Brialmont and Gleig's Life of the Duke of Wellington. 4 vols. 8vo. with Illustrations, £2 14s.

Life of the Duke of Wellington, partly from the French of M. BRIALMONT, partly from Original Documents. By the Rev. G. R. GLEIG, M.A. 8vo. with Portrait, 15s.

**History of my Religious Opinions.** By J. H. NEWMAN, D.D. Being the Substance of Apologia pro Vitâ Suâ. Post 8vo. 6s.

**Father Mathew: a Biography.** By JOHN FRANCIS MAGUIRE, M.P. Popular Edition, with Portrait. Crown 8vo. 3s. 6d.

Rome; its Rulers and its Institutions. By the same Author. New Edition in preparation.

**Memoirs, Miscellanies, and Letters** of the late Lucy Aikin; including those addressed to Dr. Channing from 1826 to 1842. Edited by P. H. LE BRETON. Post 8vo. 8s. 6d.

**Life of Amelia Wilhelmina Sieveking,** from the German. Edited, with the Author's sanction, by CATHERINE WINKWORTH. Post 8vo. with Portrait, 12s.

**Louis Spohr's Autobiography.** Translated from the German. 8vo. 14s.

**Felix Mendelssohn's Letters from** *Italy and Switzerland,* and *Letters from* 1833 *to* 1847, translated by Lady WALLACE. New Edition, with Portrait. 2 vols. crown 8vo. 5s. each.

**Diaries of a Lady of Quality,** from 1797 to 1844. Edited, with Notes, by A. HAYWARD, Q.C. Post 8vo. 10s. 6d.

**Recollections of the late William** Wilberforce, M.P. for the County of York during nearly 30 Years. By J. S. HARFORD, F.R.S. Second Edition. Post 8vo. 7s.

**Memoirs of Sir Henry Havelock,** K.C.B. By JOHN CLARK MARSHMAN. Second Edition. 8vo. with Portrait, 12s. 6d.

**Thomas Moore's Memoirs, Journal, and Correspondence.** Edited and abridged from the First Edition by Earl RUSSELL. Square crown 8vo. with 8 Portraits, 12s. 6d.

**Memoir of the Rev. Sydney Smith.**
By his Daughter, Lady HOLLAND. With a Selection from his Letters, edited by Mrs. AUSTIN. 2 vols. 8vo. 28s.

**Vicissitudes of Families.** By Sir BERNARD BURKE, Ulster King of Arms. FIRST, SECOND, and THIRD SERIES. 3 vols. crown 8vo. 12s. 6d. each.

**Essays in Ecclesiastical Biography.** By the Right Hon. Sir J. STEPHEN, LL.D. Fourth Edition. 8vo. 14s.

**Biographical Sketches.** By NASSAU W. SENIOR. Post 8vo. 10s. 6d.

**Biographies of Distinguished Scientific Men.** By FRANÇOIS ARAGO. Translated by Admiral W. H. SMYTH, F.R.S. the Rev. B. POWELL, M.A. and R. GRANT, M.A. 8vo. 18s.

**Maunder's Biographical Treasury:** Memoirs, Sketches, and Brief Notices of above 12,000 Eminent Persons of All Ages and Nations. Fcp. 8vo. 10s.

## *Criticism, Philosophy, Polity, &c.*

**Papinian:** a Dialogue on State Affairs between a Constitutional Lawyer and a Country Gentleman about to enter Public Life. By GEORGE ATKINSON, B.A. Oxon. Serjeant-at-Law. Post 8vo. 5s.

**On Representative Government.** By JOHN STUART MILL. Third Edition 8vo. 9s. crown 8vo. 2s.

**On Liberty.** By the same Author. Third Edition. Post 8vo. 7s. 6d. crown 8vo. 1s. 4d.

**Principles of Political Economy.** By the same. Sixth Edition. 2 vols. 8vo. 30s. or in 1 vol. crown 8vo. 5s.

**A System of Logic, Ratiocinative and Inductive.** By the same. Fifth Edition. 2 vols. 8vo. 25s.

**Utilitarianism.** By the same. 2d Edit. 8vo. 5s.

**Dissertations and Discussions.** By the same Author. 2 vols. 8vo. 24s.

**Examination of Sir W. Hamilton's Philosophy,** and of the Principal Philosophical Questions discussed in his Writings. By the same Author. 8vo. 14s.

**Lord Bacon's Works, collected** and edited by R. L. ELLIS, M.A. J. SPEDDING, M.A. and D. D. HEATH. VOLS. I. to V. *Philosophical Works,* 5 vols. 8vo. £4 6s. VOLS. VI. and VII. *Literary and Professional Works,* 2 vols. £1 16s.

**Bacon's Essays, with Annotations.** By R. WHATELY, D.D. late Archbishop of Dublin. Sixth Edition. 8vo. 10s. 6d.

**Elements of Logic.** By R. WHATELY, D.D. late Archbishop of Dublin. Ninth Edition. 8vo. 10s. 6d. crown 8vo. 4s. 6d.

**Elements of Rhetoric.** By the same Author. Seventh Edition. 8vo. 10s. 6d. crown 8vo. 4s. 6d.

**English Synonymes.** Edited by Archbishop WHATELY. 5th Edition. Fcp. 3s.

**Miscellaneous Remains from the** Common-place Book of RICHARD WHATELY, D.D. late Archbishop of Dublin. Edited by Miss E. J. WHATELY. Post 8vo. 7s. 6d.

**Essays on the Administrations of** Great Britain from 1783 to 1830. By the Right Hon. Sir G. C. LEWIS, Bart. Edited by the Right Hon. Sir E. HEAD, Bart. 8vo. with Portrait, 15s.

*By the same Author.*

**A Dialogue on the Best Form of** Government, 4s. 6d.

**Essay on the Origin and Formation of** the Romance Languages, 7s. 6d.

**Historical Survey of the Astronomy of** the Ancients, 15s.

**Inquiry into the Credibility of the** Early Roman History, 2 vols. 30s.

**On the Methods of Observation and** Reasoning in Politics, 2 vols. 28s.

**Irish Disturbances and Irish Church** Question, 12s.

**Remarks on the Use and Abuse of** some Political Terms, 9s.

**On Foreign Jurisdiction and Extradition of Criminals,** 2s. 6d.

**The Fables of Babrius, Greek Text** with Latin Notes, PART I. 5s. 6d. PART II. 3s. 6d.

**Suggestions for the Application of the** Egyptological Method to Modern History, 1s.

**An Outline of the Necessary** Laws of Thought: a Treatise on Pure and Applied Logic. By the Most Rev. W. THOMSON, D.D. Archbishop of York. Crown 8vo. 5s. 6d.

**The Elements of Logic.** By THOMAS SHEDDEN, M.A. of St. Peter's Coll. Cantab. 12mo. 4s. 6d.

**Analysis of Mr. Mill's System of Logic.** By W. STEBBING, M.A. Fellow of Worcester College, Oxford. 12mo. 3s. 6d.

**The Election of Representatives,** Parliamentary and Municipal; a Treatise. By THOMAS HARE, Barrister-at-Law. Third Edition, with Additions. Crown 8vo. 6s.

**Speeches of the Right Hon. Lord** MACAULAY, corrected by Himself. 8vo. 12s.

**Lord Macaulay's Speeches on** Parliamentary Reform in 1831 and 1832. 16mo. 1s.

**A Dictionary of the English Language.** By R. G. LATHAM, M.A. M.D. F.R.S. Founded on the Dictionary of Dr. S. JOHNSON, as edited by the Rev. H. J. TODD, with numerous Emendations and Additions. Publishing in 36 Parts, price 3s. 6d. each, to form 2 vols. 4to.

**Thesaurus of English Words and** Phrases, classified and arranged so as to facilitate the Expression of Ideas, and assist in Literary Composition. By P. M. ROGET, M.D. 14th Edition, crown 8vo. 10s. 6d.

**Lectures on the Science of Language,** delivered at the Royal Institution. By MAX MÜLLER, M.A. Taylorian Professor in the University of Oxford. FIRST SERIES, Fourth Edition, 12s. SECOND SERIES, 18s.

**The Debater;** a Series of Complete Debates, Outlines of Debates, and Questions for Discussion. By F. ROWTON. Fcp. 6s.

**A Course of English Reading,** adapted to every taste and capacity; or, How and What to Read. By the Rev. J. PYCROFT, B.A. Fourth Edition, fcp. 5s.

**Manual of English Literature,** Historical and Critical: with a Chapter on English Metres. By THOMAS ARNOLD, B.A. Post 8vo. 10s. 6d.

**Southey's Doctor,** complete in One Volume. Edited by the Rev. J.W. WARTER, B.D. Square crown 8vo. 12s. 6d.

**Historical and Critical Commentary** on the Old Testament; with a New Translation. By M. M. KALISCH, Ph. D. VOL. I. Genesis, 8vo. 18s. or adapted for the General Reader, 12s. VOL. II. Exodus, 15s. or adapted for the General Reader, 12s.

**A Hebrew Grammar, with Exercises.** By the same. PART I. Outlines with Exercises, 8vo. 12s. 6d. KEY, 5s. PART II. Exceptional Forms and Constructions, 12s. 6d.

**A Latin-English Dictionary.** By J. T. WHITE, M.A. of Corpus Christi College, and J. E. RIDDLE, M.A. of St. Edmund Hall, Oxford. Imp. 8vo. pp. 2,128, 42s.

**A New Latin-English Dictionary,** abridged from the larger work of *White* and *Riddle* (as above), by J. T. WHITE, M.A. Joint-Author. Medium 8vo. pp. 1,018, 18s.

**A Diamond Latin-English Dictionary,** or Guide to the Meaning, Quality, and Accentuation of Latin Classical Words. By J. E. RIDDLE, M.A. 32mo. 2s. 6d.

**An English-Greek Lexicon,** containing all the Greek Words used by Writers of good authority. By C. D. YONGE, B.A. Fifth Edition. 4to. 21s.

**Mr. Yonge's New Lexicon, English** and Greek, abridged from his larger work (as above). Square 12mo. 8s. 6d.

**A Greek-English Lexicon.** Compiled by H. G. LIDDELL, D.D. Dean of Christ Church, and R. SCOTT, D.D. Master of Balliol. Fifth Edition, crown 4to. 31s. 6d.

**A Lexicon, Greek and English,** abridged from LIDDELL and SCOTT's *Greek-English Lexicon*. Eleventh Edition, square 12mo. 7s. 6d.

**A Practical Dictionary of the** French and English Languages. By L. CONTANSEAU. 8th Edition, post 8vo. 10s. 6d.

**Contanseau's Pocket Dictionary,** French and English, abridged from the above by the Author. New Edition. 18mo. 5s.

**New Practical Dictionary of the** German Language; German-English, and English-German. By the Rev. W. L. BLACKLEY, M.A., and Dr. CARL MARTIN FRIEDLANDER. Post 8vo. [*In the press.*

## Miscellaneous Works and Popular Metaphysics.

**Recreations of a Country Parson:** being a Selection of the Contributions of A. K. H. B. to *Fraser's Magazine*. SECOND SERIES. Crown 8vo. 3s. 6d.

**The Commonplace Philosopher in Town and Country.** By the same Author. Crown 8vo. 3s 6d.

**Leisure Hours in Town;** Essays Consolatory, Æsthetical, Moral, Social, and Domestic. By the same. Crown 8vo. 3s. 6d.

**The Autumn Holidays of a Country Parson:** Essays contributed to *Fraser's Magazine* and to *Good Words*, by the same. Crown 8vo. 3s. 6d.

**The Graver Thoughts of a Country Parson,** SECOND SERIES. By the same. Crown 8vo. 3s. 6d.

**Critical Essays of a Country Parson,** selected from Essays contributed to *Fraser's Magazine*, by the same. Post 8vo. 9s.

**A Campaigner at Home.** By SHIRLEY, Author of 'Thalatta' and 'Nugæ Criticæ.' Post 8vo. with Vignette, 7s. 6d.

**Friends in Council:** a Series of Readings and Discourses thereon. 2 vols. fcp. 9s.

**Friends in Council,** SECOND SERIES. 2 vols. post 8vo. 14s.

**Essays written in the Intervals of Business.** Fcp. 2s. 6d.

**Lord Macaulay's Miscellaneous Writings.**
LIBRARY EDITION, 2 vols. 8vo. Portrait, 21s.
PEOPLE'S EDITION, 1 vol. crown 8vo. 4s. 6d.

**The Rev. Sydney Smith's Miscellaneous Works;** including his Contributions to the *Edinburgh Review*.
LIBRARY EDITION, 3 vols. 8vo. 36s.
TRAVELLER'S EDITION, in 1 vol. 21s.
In POCKET VOLUMES, 3 vols. fcp. 21s.
PEOPLE'S EDITION, 2 vols. crown 8vo. 8s.

**Elementary Sketches of Moral Philosophy,** delivered at the Royal Institution. By the same Author. Fcp. 7s.

**The Wit and Wisdom of the Rev. SYDNEY SMITH:** a Selection of the most memorable Passages in his Writings and Conversation. 16mo. 7s. 6d.

**The History of the Supernatural** in All Ages and Nations, and in All Churches, Christian and Pagan; demonstrating a Universal Faith. By WILLIAM HOWITT. 2 vols. post 8vo. 18s.

**The Superstitions of Witchcraft.** By HOWARD WILLIAMS, M.A. St. John's Coll. Camb. Post 8vo. 7s. 6d.

**Chapters on Mental Physiology.** By Sir HENRY HOLLAND, Bart. M.D. F.R.S. Second Edition. Post 8vo. 8s. 6d.

**Essays selected from Contributions to the *Edinburgh Review*.** By HENRY ROGERS. Second Edition. 3 vols. fcp. 21s.

**The Eclipse of Faith;** or, a Visit to a Religious Sceptic. By the same Author. Tenth Edition. Fcp. 5s.

**Defence of the Eclipse of Faith,** by its Author; a Rejoinder to Dr. Newman's *Reply*. Third Edition. Fcp. 3s. 6d.

**Selections from the Correspondence of R. E. H. Greyson.** By the same Author. Third Edition. Crown 8vo. 7s. 6d.

**Fulleriana, or the Wisdom and Wit of THOMAS FULLER,** with Essay on his Life and Genius. By the same Author. 16mo. 2s. 6d.

**The Secret of Hegel:** being the Hegelian System in Origin, Principle, Form, and Matter. By JAMES HUTCHISON STIRLING. 2 vols. 8vo. 28s.

**An Introduction to Mental Philosophy,** on the Inductive Method. By J. D. MORELL, M.A. LL.D. 8vo. 12s.

**Elements of Psychology,** containing the Analysis of the Intellectual Powers. By the same Author. Post 8vo. 7s. 6d.

**Sight and Touch:** an Attempt to Disprove the Received (or Berkeleian) Theory of Vision. By THOMAS K. ABBOTT, M.A. Fellow and Tutor of Trin. Coll. Dublin. 8vo. with 21 Woodcuts, 5s. 6d.

**The Senses and the Intellect.** By ALEXANDER BAIN, M.A. Prof. of Logic in the Univ. of Aberdeen. Second Edition. 8vo. 15s.

**The Emotions and the Will,** by the same Author; completing a Systematic Exposition of the Human Mind. 8vo. 15s.

**On the Study of Character,** including an Estimate of Phrenology. By the same Author. 8vo. 9s.

**Time and Space:** a Metaphysical Essay. By SHADWORTH H. HODGSON. 8vo. pp. 588, price 16s.

**Hours with the Mystics:** a Contribution to the History of Religious Opinion. By ROBERT ALFRED VAUGHAN, B.A. Second Edition. 2 vols. crown 8vo. 12s.

**Psychological Inquiries.** By the late Sir BENJ. C. BRODIE, Bart. 2 vols. or SERIES, fcp. 5s. each.

**The Philosophy of Necessity**; or, Natural Law as applicable to Mental, Moral, and Social Science. By CHARLES BRAY. Second Edition. 8vo. 9s.

**The Education of the Feelings and Affections.** By the same Author. Third Edition. 8vo. 3s. 6d.

**Christianity and Common Sense.** By Sir WILLOUGHBY JONES, Bart. M.A. Trin. Coll. Cantab. 8vo. 6s.

---

## *Astronomy, Meteorology, Popular Geography, &c.*

**Outlines of Astronomy.** By Sir J. F. W. HERSCHEL, Bart, M.A. Seventh Edition, revised; with Plates and Woodcuts. 8vo. 18s.

**Arago's Popular Astronomy.** Translated by Admiral W. H. SMYTH, F.R.S. and R. GRANT, M.A. With 25 Plates and 358 Woodcuts. 2 vols. 8vo. £2 5s.

**Arago's Meteorological Essays,** with Introduction by Baron HUMBOLDT. Translated under the superintendence of Major-General E. SABINE, R.A. 8vo. 18s.

**Saturn and its System.** By RICHARD A. PROCTOR, B.A. late Scholar of St. John's Coll. Camb. and King's Coll. London. 8vo. with 14 Plates, 14s.

**The Weather-Book;** a Manual of Practical Meteorology. By Rear-Admiral ROBERT FITZ ROY, R.N. F.R.S. Third Edition, with 16 Diagrams. 8vo. 15s.

**Saxby's Weather System,** or Lunar Influence on Weather. By S. M. SAXBY, R..N. Instructor of Naval Engineers. Second Edition. Post 8vo. 4s.

**Dove's Law of Storms** considered in connexion with the ordinary Movements of the Atmosphere. Translated by R. H. SCOTT, M.A. T.C.D. 8vo. 10s. 6d.

**Celestial Objects for Common Telescopes.** By T. W. WEBB, M.A. F.R.A.S. With Map of the Moon, and Woodcuts. 16mo. 7s.

**Physical Geography for Schools** and General Readers. By M. F. MAURY, LL.D. Fcp. with 2 Charts, 2s. 6d.

**A Dictionary, Geographical, Statistical, and Historical,** of the various Countries, Places, and principal Natural Objects in the World. By J. R. M'CULLOCH. With 6 Maps. 2 vols. 8vo. 63s.

**A General Dictionary of Geography,** Descriptive, Physical, Statistical, and Historical; forming a complete Gazetteer of the World. By A. KEITH JOHNSTON, F.R.S.E. 8vo. 31s. 6d,

**A Manual of Geography,** Physical, Industrial, and Political. By W. HUGHES, F.R.G.S. Prof. of Geog. in King's Coll. and in Queen's Coll. Lond. With 6 Maps. Fcp. 7s. 6d.

**The Geography of British History;** a Geographical Description of the British Islands at Successive Periods. By the same. With 6 Maps. Fcp. 8s. 6d.

**Abridged Text-Book of British Geography.** By the same. Fcp. 1s. 6d.

**The British Empire;** a Sketch of the Geography, Growth, Natural and Political Features of the United Kingdom, its Colonies and Dependencies. By CAROLINE BRAY. With 5 Maps. Fcp. 7s. 6d.

**Colonisation and Colonies:** a Series of Lectures delivered before the University of Oxford. By HERMAN MERIVALE, M.A. Prof. of Polit. Econ. 8vo. 18s.

**Maunder's Treasury of Geography,** Physical, Historical, Descriptive, and Political. Edited by W. HUGHES, F.R.G.S. With 7 Maps and 16 Plates. Fcp. 10s.

## Natural History and Popular Science.

**The Elements of Physics or** Natural Philosophy. By NEIL ARNOTT, M.D. F.R.S. Physician Extraordinary to the Queen. Sixth Edition. PART I. 8vo. 10s. 6d.

**Heat Considered as a Mode of Motion.** By Professor JOHN TYNDALL, F.R.S. LL.D. Second Edition. Crown 8vo. with Woodcuts, 12s. 6d.

**Volcanos,** the Character of their Phenomena, their Share in the Structure and Composition of the Surface of the Globe, &c. By G. POULETT SCROPE, M.P. F.R.S. Second Edition. 8vo. with Illustrations, 15s.

**A Treatise on Electricity,** in Theory and Practice. By A. DE LA RIVE, Prof. in the Academy of Geneva. Translated by C. V. WALKER, F.R.S. 3 vols. 8vo. with Woodcuts, £3 13s.

**The Correlation of Physical Forces.** By W. R. GROVE, Q.C. V.P.R.S. Fourth Edition. 8vo. 7s. 6d.

**The Geological Magazine;** or, Monthly Journal of Geology. Edited by HENRY WOODWARD, F.G.S. F.Z.S. British Museum; assisted by Professor J. MORRIS, F.G.S. and R. ETHERIDGE, F.R.S.E. F.G.S. 8vo. price 1s. monthly.

**A Guide to Geology.** By J. PHILLIPS, M.A. Prof. of Geol. in the Univ. of Oxford. Fifth Edition; with Plates and Diagrams. Fcp. 4s.

**A Glossary of Mineralogy.** By H. W. BRISTOW, F.G.S. of the Geological Survey of Great Britain. With 486 Figures. Crown 8vo. 12s.

**Phillips's Elementary Introduction** to Mineralogy, with extensive Alterations and Additions, by H. J. BROOKE, F.R.S. and W. H. MILLER, F.G.S. Post 8vo. with Woodcuts, 18s.

**Van Der Hoeven's Handbook of** ZOOLOGY. Translated from the Second Dutch Edition by the Rev. W. CLARK, M.D. F.R.S. 2 vols. 8vo. with 24 Plates of Figures, 60s.

**The Comparative Anatomy and** Physiology of the Vertebrate Animals. By RICHARD OWEN, F.R.S. D.C.L. 2 vols. 8vo. with upwards of 1,200 Woodcuts.
[*In the press.*

**Homes without Hands:** an Account of the Habitations constructed by various Animals, classed according to their Principles of Construction. By Rev. J. G. WOOD, M.A. F.L.S. Illustrations on Wood by G. Pearson, from Drawings by F. W. Keyl and E. A. Smith. In 20 Parts, 1s. each.

**Manual of Corals and Sea Jellies.** By J. R. GREENE, B.A. Edited by the Rev. J. A. GALBRAITH, M.A. and the Rev. S. HAUGHTON, M.D. Fcp. with 39 Woodcuts, 5s.

**Manual of Sponges and Animalculæ;** with a General Introduction on the Principles of Zoology. By the same Author and Editors. Fcp. with 16 Woodcuts, 2s.

**Manual of the Metalloids.** By J. APJOHN, M.D. F.R.S. and the same Editors. Fcp. with 38 Woodcuts, 7s. 6d.

**The Sea and its Living Wonders.** By Dr. G. HARTWIG. Second (English) Edition. 8vo. with many Illustrations, 18s.

**The Tropical World.** By the same Author. With 8 Chromoxylographs and 172 Woodcuts. 8vo. 21s.

**Sketches of the Natural History** of Ceylon. By Sir J. EMERSON TENNENT, K.C.S. LL.D. With 82 Wood Engravings. Post 8vo. 12s. 6d.

**Ceylon.** By the same Author. 5th Edition; with Maps, &c. and 90 Wood Engravings. 2 vols. 8vo. £2 10s.

**A Familiar History of Birds.** By E. STANLEY, D.D. F.R.S. late Lord Bishop of Norwich. Seventh Edition, with Woodcuts. Fcp. 3s. 6d.

**Marvels and Mysteries of Instinct;** or, Curiosities of Animal Life. By G. GARRATT. Third Edition. Fcp. 7s.

**Home Walks and Holiday Rambles.** By the Rev. C. A. JOHNS, B.A. F.L.S. Fcp. with 10 Illustrations, 6s.

# NEW WORKS published by LONGMANS and CO.   9

**Kirby and Spence's Introduction**
to Entomology, or Elements of the Natural History of Insects. Seventh Edition. Crown 8vo. 5s.

**Maunder's Treasury of Natural**
History, or Popular Dictionary of Zoology. Revised and corrected by T. S. COBBOLD, M.D. Fcp. with 900 Woodcuts, 10s.

**The Treasury of Botany, on the**
Plan of Maunder's Treasury. By J. LINDLEY, M.D. and T. MOORE, F.L.S. assisted by other Practical Botanists. With 16 Plates, and many Woodcuts from designs by W. H. Fitch. Fcp. [*In the press.*

**The Rose Amateur's Guide.** By THOMAS RIVERS. 8th Edition. Fcp. 4s.

**The British Flora;** comprising the Phænogamous or Flowering Plants and the Ferns. By Sir W. J. HOOKER, K.H. and G. A. WALKER-ARNOTT, LL.D. 12mo. with 12 Plates, 14s. or coloured, 21s.

**Bryologia Britannica;** containing the Mosses of Great Britain and Ireland, arranged and described. By W. WILSON. 8vo. with 61 Plates, 42s. or coloured, £4 4s.

**The Indoor Gardener.** By Miss MALING. Fcp. with Frontispiece, 5s.

**Loudon's Encyclopædia of Plants;**
comprising the Specific Character, Description, Culture, History, &c. of all the Plants found in Great Britain. With upwards of 12,000 Woodcuts. 8vo. £3 13s. 6d.

**Loudon's Encyclopædia of Trees and**
Shrubs; containing the Hardy Trees and Shrubs of Great Britain scientifically and popularly described. With 2,000 Woodcuts. 8vo. 50s.

**Maunder's Scientific and Literary Treasury;** a Popular Encyclopædia of Science, Literature, and Art. Fcp. 10s.

**A Dictionary of Science, Literature, and Art.** Fourth Edition. Edited by W. T. BRANDE, D.C.L. and GEORGE W. Cox, M.A., assisted by gentlemen of eminent Scientific and Literary Acquirements. In 12 Parts, each containing 240 pages, price 5s. forming 3 vols. medium 8vo. price 21s. each.

**Essays on Scientific and other**
subjects, contributed to Reviews. By Sir H. HOLLAND, Bart. M.D. Second Edition. 8vo. 14s.

**Essays from the Edinburgh and**
*Quarterly Reviews;* with Addresses and other Pieces. By Sir J. F. W. HERSCHEL, Bart. M.A. 8vo. 18s.

---

*Chemistry, Medicine, Surgery, and the Allied Sciences.*

**A Dictionary of Chemistry and**
the Allied Branches of other Sciences. By HENRY WATTS, F.C.S. assisted by eminent Contributors. 5 vols. medium 8vo. in course of publication in Parts. VOL. I. 3s. 6d. VOL. II. 26s. and VOL. III. 31s. 6d. are now ready.

**Handbook of Chemical Analysis,**
adapted to the Unitary System of Notation: By F. T. CONINGTON, M.A. F.C.S. Post 8vo. 7s. 6d.—TABLES of QUALITATIVE ANALYSIS adapted to the same, 2s. 6d.

**A Handbook of Volumetrical**
Analysis. By ROBERT H. SCOTT, M.A. T.C.D. Post 8vo. 4s. 6d.

**Elements of Chemistry, Theoretical and Practical.** By WILLIAM A. MILLER, M.D. LL.D. F.R.S. F.G.S. Professor of Chemistry, King's College, London. 3 vols. 8vo. £2 13s. PART I. CHEMICAL PHYSICS, Third Edition, 12s. PART II. INORGANIC CHEMISTRY, 21s. PART III. ORGANIC CHEMISTRY, Second Edition, 20s.

**A Manual of Chemistry,** Descriptive and Theoretical. By WILLIAM ODLING, M.B. F.R.S. Lecturer on Chemistry at St. Bartholomew's Hospital. PART I. 8vo. 9s.

**A Course of Practical Chemistry,** for the use of Medical Students. By the same Author. Second Edition, with 70 new Woodcuts. Crown 8vo. 7s. 6d.

**The Diagnosis and Treatment of**
the Diseases of Women; including the Diagnosis of Pregnancy. By GRAILY HEWITT, M.D. Physician to the British Lying-in Hospital. 8vo. 16s.

**Lectures on the Diseases of Infancy** and Childhood. By CHARLES WEST, M.D. &c. 5th Edition, revised and enlarged. 8vo. 16s.

**Exposition of the Signs and**
Symptoms of Pregnancy: with other Papers on subjects connected with Midwifery. By W. F. MONTGOMERY, M.A. M.D. M.R.I.A. 8vo. with Illustrations, 25s.

B

**A System of Surgery, Theoretical and Practical,** in Treatises by Various Authors. Edited by T. HOLMES, M.A. Cantab. Assistant-Surgeon to St. George's Hospital. 4 vols. 8vo. £4 13s.

Vol. I. General Pathology, 21s.

Vol. II. Local Injuries: Gun-shot Wounds, Injuries of the Head, Back, Face, Neck, Chest, Abdomen, Pelvis, of the Upper and Lower Extremities, and Diseases of the Eye. 21s.

Vol. III. Operative Surgery. Diseases of the Organs of Circulation, Locomotion, &c. 21s.

Vol. IV. Diseases of the Organs of Digestion, of the Genito-Urinary System, and of the Breast, Thyroid Gland, and Skin; with APPENDIX and GENERAL INDEX. 30s.

**Lectures on the Principles and Practice of Physic.** By THOMAS WATSON, M.D. Physician-Extraordinary to the Queen. Fourth Edition. 2 vols. 8vo. 34s.

**Lectures on Surgical Pathology.** By J. PAGET, F.R.S. Surgeon-Extraordinary to the Queen. Edited by W. TURNER, M.B. 8vo. with 117 Woodcuts, 21s.

**A Treatise on the Continued Fevers of Great Britain.** By C. MURCHISON, M.D. Senior Physician to the London Fever Hospital. 8vo. with coloured Plates, 18s.

**Anatomy, Descriptive and Surgical.** By HENRY GRAY, F.R.S. With 410 Wood Engravings from Dissections. Third Edition, by T. HOLMES, M.A. Cantab. Royal 8vo. 28s.

**The Cyclopædia of Anatomy and Physiology.** Edited by the late R. B. TODD, M.D. F.R.S. Assisted by nearly all the most eminent cultivators of Physiological Science of the present age. 5 vols. 8vo. with 2,853 Woodcuts, £6 6s.

**Physiological Anatomy and Physiology of Man.** By the late R. B. TODD, M.D. F.R.S. and W. BOWMAN, F.R.S. of King's College. With numerous Illustrations. VOL. II. 8vo. 25s.

**A Dictionary of Practical Medicine.** By J. COPLAND, M.D. F.R.S. Abridged from the larger work by the Author, assisted by J. C. COPLAND, M.R.C.S. 1 vol. 8vo. [*In the press.*

Dr. Copland's Dictionary of Practical Medicine (the larger work). 3 vols. 8vo. £5 11s.

**The Works of Sir B. C. Brodie,** Bart. collected and arranged by CHARLES HAWKINS, F.R.C.S.E. 3 vols. 8vo. with Medallion and Facsimile, 48s.

**Autobiography of Sir B. C. Brodie,** Bart. printed from the Author's materials left in MS. Fcp. 4s. 6d.

**Medical Notes and Reflections.** By Sir H. HOLLAND, Bart. M.D. Third Edition. 8vo. 18s.

**A Manual of Materia Medica** and Therapeutics, abridged from Dr. PEREIRA's *Elements* by F. J. FARRE, M.D. Cantab. assisted by R. BENTLEY, M.R.C.S. and by R. WARINGTON, F.C.S. 1 vol. 8vo. [*In October.*

Dr. Pereira's Elements of Materia Medica and Therapeutics, Third Edition, by A. S. TAYLOR, M.D. and G. O. REES, M.D. 3 vols. 8vo. with Woodcuts, £3 15s.

**Thomson's Conspectus of the British Pharmacopœia.** Twenty-fourth Edition, corrected and made conformable throughout to the New Pharmacopœia of the General Council of Medical Education. By E. LLOYD BIRKETT, M.D. 18mo. 5s. 6d.

**Manual of the Domestic Practice of Medicine.** By W. B. KESTEVEN, F.R.C.S.E. Second Edition, thoroughly revised, with Additions. Fcp. 5s.

---

*The Fine Arts, and Illustrated Editions.*

**The New Testament,** illustrated with Wood Engravings after the Early Masters, chiefly of the Italian School. Crown 4to. 63s. cloth, gilt top; or £5 5s. elegantly bound in morocco.

**Lyra Germanica;** Hymns for the Sundays and Chief Festivals of the Christian Year. Translated by CATHERINE WINKWORTH; 125 Illustrations on Wood drawn by J. LEIGHTON, F.S.A. Fcp. 4to. 21s.

**Cats' and Farlie's Moral Emblems**; with Aphorisms, Adages, and Proverbs of all Nations: comprising 121 Illustrations on Wood by J. LEIGHTON, F.S.A. with an appropriate Text by R. PIGOT. Imperial 8vo. 31s. 6d.

**Bunyan's Pilgrim's Progress**: with 126 Illustrations on Steel and Wood by C. BENNETT; and a Preface by the Rev. C. KINGSLEY. Fcp. 4to. 21s.

**Shakspeare's Sentiments and Similes** printed in Black and Gold and illuminated in the Missal style by HENRY NOEL HUMPHREYS. In massive covers, containing the Medallion and Cypher of Shakspeare. Square post 8vo. 21s.

**The History of Our Lord**, as exemplified in Works of Art; with that of His Types in the Old and New Testament. By Mrs. JAMESON and Lady EASTLAKE. Being the concluding Series of 'Sacred and Legendary Art;' with 13 Etchings and 281 Woodcuts. 2 vols. square crown 8vo. 42s.

*In the same Series, by Mrs. JAMESON.*

**Legends of the Saints and Martyrs.** Fourth Edition, with 19 Etchings and 187 Woodcuts. 2 vols. 31s. 6d.

**Legends of the Monastic Orders.** Third Edition, with 11 Etchings and 88 Woodcuts. 1 vol. 21s.

**Legends of the Madonna.** Third Edition. with 27 Etchings and 165 Woodcuts. 1 vol. 21s.

## Arts, Manufactures, &c.

**Encyclopædia of Architecture,** Historical, Theoretical, and Practical. By JOSEPH GWILT. With more than 1,000 Woodcuts. 8vo. 42s.

**Tuscan Sculptors, their Lives,** Works, and Times. With 45 Etchings and 28 Woodcuts from Original Drawings and Photographs. By CHARLES C. PERKINS 2 vols. imp. 8vo. 63s.

**The Engineer's Handbook;** explaining the Principles which should guide the young Engineer in the Construction of Machinery. By C. S. LOWNDES. Post 8vo. 5s.

**The Elements of Mechanism.** By T. M. GOODEVE, M.A. Prof. of Mechanics at the R.M. Acad. Woolwich. Second Edition, with 217 Woodcuts. Post 8vo. 6s. 6d.

**Ure's Dictionary of Arts, Manufactures, and Mines.** Re-written and enlarged by ROBERT HUNT, F.R.S., assisted by numerous gentlemen eminent in Science and the Arts. With 2,000 Woodcuts. 3 vols. 8vo. £4.

**Encyclopædia of Civil Engineering,** Historical, Theoretical, and Practical. By E. CRESY, C.E. With above 3,000 Woodcuts. 8vo. 42s.

**Treatise on Mills and Millwork.** By W. FAIRBAIRN, C.E. F.R.S. With 18 Plates and 322 Woodcuts. 2 vols. 8vo. 32s.

**Useful Information for Engineers.** By the same Author. FIRST and SECOND SERIES, with many Plates and Woodcuts. 2 vols. crown 8vo. 10s. 6d. each.

**The Application of Cast and Wrought Iron to Building Purposes.** By the same Author. Third Edition, with 6 Plates and 118 Woodcuts. 8vo. 16s.

**The Practical Mechanic's Journal:** An Illustrated Record of Mechanical and Engineering Science, and Epitome of Patent Inventions. 4to. price 1s. monthly.

**The Practical Draughtsman's Book of Industrial Design.** By W. JOHNSON, Assoc. Inst. C.E. With many hundred Illustrations. 4to. 28s. 6d.

**The Patentee's Manual:** a Treatise on the Law and Practice of Letters Patent for the use of Patentees and Inventors. By J. and J. H. JOHNSON. Post 8vo. 7s. 6d.

**The Artisan Club's Treatise on the Steam Engine,** in its various Applications to Mines, Mills, Steam Navigation, Railways, and Agriculture. By J. BOURNE, C.E. Sixth Edition; with 37 Plates and 546 Woodcuts. 4to. 42s.

**Catechism of the Steam Engine,** in its various Applications to Mines, Mills, Steam Navigation, Railways, and Agriculture. By J. BOURNE, C.E. With 199 Woodcuts. Fcp. 9s. The INTRODUCTION of 'Recent Improvements' may be had separately, with 110 Woodcuts, price 3s. 6d.

**Handbook of the Steam Engine,** by the same Author, forming a KEY to the Catechism of the Steam Engine, with 67 Woodcuts. Fcp. 9s.

**The Theory of War Illustrated** by numerous Examples from History. By Lieut.-Col. P. L. MACDOUGALL. Third Edition, with 10 Plans. Post 8vo. 10s. 6d.

**Collieries and Colliers;** A Handbook of the Law and leading Cases relating thereto. By J. C. FOWLER, Barrister-at-Law, Stipendiary Magistrate. Fcp. 6s.

**The Art of Perfumery;** the History and Theory of Odours, and the Methods of Extracting the Aromas of Plants. By Dr. PIESSE, F.C.S. Third Edition, with 53 Woodcuts. Crown 8vo. 10s. 6d.

**Chemical, Natural, and Physical Magic,** for Juveniles during the Holidays. By the same Author. Third Edition, enlarged, with 38 Woodcuts. Fcp. 6s.

**The Laboratory of Chemical Wonders:** A Scientific Mélange for Young People. By the same. Crown 8vo. 5s. 6d.

**Talpa;** or, the Chronicles of a Clay Farm. By C. W. HOSKYNS, Esq. With 24 Woodcuts from Designs by G. CRUIKSHANK. 16mo. 5s. 6d.

**H.R.H. the Prince Consort's** Farms; an Agricultural Memoir. By JOHN CHALMERS MORTON. Dedicated by permission to Her Majesty the QUEEN. With 40 Wood Engravings. 4to. 52s. 6d.

**Loudon's Encyclopædia of Agriculture:** Comprising the Laying-out, Improvement, and Management of Landed Property, and the Cultivation and Economy of the Productions of Agriculture. With 1,100 Woodcuts. 8vo. 31s. 6d.

**Loudon's Encyclopædia of Gardening:** Comprising the Theory and Practice of Horticulture, Floriculture, Arboriculture, and Landscape Gardening. With 1,000 Woodcuts. 8vo. 31s. 6d.

**Loudon's Encyclopædia of Cottage, Farm,** and Villa Architecture and Furniture. With more than 2,000 Woodcuts. 8vo. 42s.

**History of Windsor Great Park** and Windsor Forest. By WILLIAM MENZIES, Resident Deputy Surveyor. With 2 Maps and 20 Photographs. Imp. folio, £8 8s.

**The Sanitary Management and Utilisation of Sewage:** comprising Details of a System applicable to Cottages, Dwelling-Houses, Public Buildings, and Towns; Suggestions relating to the Arterial Drainage of the Country, and the Water Supply of Rivers. By the same Author. Imp. 8vo. with 9 Illustrations, 12s. 6d.

**Bayldon's Art of Valuing Rents** and Tillages, and Claims of Tenants upon Quitting Farms, both at Michaelmas and Lady-Day. Eighth Edition, revised by J. C. MORTON. 8vo. 10s. 6d.

---

*Religious and Moral Works.*

**An Exposition of the 39 Articles,** Historical and Doctrinal. By E. HAROLD BROWNE, D.D. Lord Bishop of Ely. Sixth Edition, 8vo. 16s.

**The Pentateuch and the Elohistic** Psalms, in Reply to Bishop Colenso. By the same. Second Edition. 8vo. 2s.

**Examination Questions on Bishop** Browne's Exposition of the Articles. By the Rev. J. GORLE, M.A. Fcp. 3s. 6d.

**Five Lectures on the Character** of St. Paul; being the Hulsean Lectures for 1862. By the Rev. J. S. HOWSON, D.D. Second Edition. 8vo. 9s.

**The Life and Epistles of St.** Paul. By W. J. CONYBEARE, M.A. late Fellow of Trin. Coll. Cantab. and J. S. HOWSON, D.D. Principal of Liverpool Coll.

LIBRARY EDITION, with all the Original Illustrations, Maps, Landscapes on Steel, Woodcuts, &c. 2 vols. 4to. 48s.

INTERMEDIATE EDITION, with a Selection of Maps, Plates, and Woodcuts. 2 vols. square crown 8vo. 31s. 6d.

PEOPLE'S EDITION, revised and condensed, with 46 Illustrations and Maps. 2 vols. crown 8vo. 12s.

**The Voyage and Shipwreck of St. Paul;** with Dissertations on the Ships and Navigation of the Ancients. By JAMES SMITH, F.R.S. Crown 8vo. Charts, 8s. 6d.

**A Critical and Grammatical Commentary on St. Paul's Epistles.** By C. J. ELLICOTT, D.D. Lord Bishop of Gloucester and Bristol. 8vo.
Galatians, Third Edition, 8s. 6d.
Ephesians, Third Edition, 8s. 6d.
Pastoral Epistles, Third Edition, 10s. 6d.
Philippians, Colossians, and Philemon, Third Edition, 10s. 6d.
Thessalonians, Second Edition, 7s. 6d.

**Historical Lectures on the Life of Our Lord Jesus Christ:** being the Hulsean Lectures for 1859. By the same Author. Fourth Edition. 8vo. 10s. 6d.

**The Destiny of the Creature;** and other Sermons preached before the University of Cambridge. By the same. Post 8vo. 5s.

**The Broad and the Narrow Way;** Two Sermons preached before the University of Cambridge. By the same. Crown 8vo. 2s.

### Rev. T. H. Horne's Introduction
to the Critical Study and Knowledge of the Holy Scriptures. Eleventh Edition, corrected, and extended under careful Editorial revision. With 4 Maps and 22 Woodcuts and Facsimiles. 4 vols. 8vo. £3 13s. 6d.

**Rev. T. H. Horne's Compendious Introduction to the Study of the Bible,** being an Analysis of the larger work by the same Author. Re-edited by the Rev. JOHN AYRE, M.A. With Maps, &c. Post 8vo. 9s.

**The Treasury of Bible Knowledge,** on the plan of Maunder's Treasuries. By the Rev. JOHN AYRE, M.A. Fcp. 8vo. with Maps and Illustrations. [*In the press.*

**The Greek Testament; with Notes,** Grammatical and Exegetical. By the Rev. W. WEBSTER, M.A. and the Rev. W. F. WILKINSON, M.A. 2 vols. 8vo. £2 4s.
VOL. I. the Gospels and Acts, 20s.
VOL. II. the Epistles and Apocalypse, 24s.

**The Four Experiments in Church and State;** and the Conflicts of Churches. By Lord ROBERT MONTAGU, M.P. 8vo. 12s.

**Every-day Scripture Difficulties** explained and illustrated; Gospels of St. Matthew and St. Mark. By J. E. PRESCOTT, M.A. 8vo. 9s.

**The Pentateuch and Book of Joshua Critically Examined.** By the Right Rev. J. W. COLENSO, D.D. Lord Bishop of Natal. People's Edition, in 1 vol. crown 8vo. 6s. or in 5 Parts, 1s. each.

**The Pentateuch and Book of Joshua Critically Examined.** By Prof. A. KUENEN, of Leyden. Translated from the Dutch, and edited with Notes, by the Right Rev. J. W. COLENSO, D.D. Bishop of Natal. 8vo. 8s. 6d.

**The Formation of Christendom.** PART I. By T. W. ALLIES. 8vo. 12s.

**Christendom's Divisions;** a Philosophical Sketch of the Divisions of the Christian Family in East and West. By EDMUND S. FFOULKES, formerly Fellow and Tutor of Jesus Coll. Oxford. Post 8vo. 7s. 6d.

**The Life of Christ,** an Eclectic Gospel, from the Old and New Testaments, arranged on a New Principle, with Analytical Tables, &c. By CHARLES DE LA PRYME, M.A. Trin. Coll. Camb. Revised Edition. 8vo. 5s.

**The Hidden Wisdom of Christ** and the Key of Knowledge; or, History of the Apocrypha. By ERNEST DE BUNSEN. 2 vols. 8vo. 28s.

**Hippolytus and his Age;** or, the Beginnings and Prospects of Christianity. By Baron BUNSEN, D.D. 2 vols. 8vo. 30s.

**Outlines of the Philosophy of Universal History,** applied to Language and Religion: Containing an Account of the Alphabetical Conferences. By the same Author. 2 vols. 8vo. 33s.

**Analecta Ante-Nicæna.** By the same Author. 3 vols. 8vo. 42s.

**Essays on Religion and Literature.** By various Writers. Edited by H. E. MANNING, D.D. 8vo. 10s. 6d.

**Essays and Reviews.** By the Rev. W. TEMPLE, D.D. the Rev. R. WILLIAMS, B.D. the Rev. B. POWELL, M.A. the Rev. H. B. WILSON, B.D. C. W. GOODWIN, M.A. the Rev. M. PATTISON, B.D. and the Rev. B. JOWETT, M.A. 12th Edition. Fcp. 8vo. 5s.

**Mosheim's Ecclesiastical History.** MURDOCK and SOAMES's Translation and Notes, re-edited by the Rev. W. STUBBS, M.A. 3 vols. 8vo. 45s.

**Bishop Jeremy Taylor's Entire Works**: With Life by BISHOP HEBER. Revised and corrected by the Rev. C. P. EDEN, 10 vols. £5 5s.

**Passing Thoughts on Religion.** By the Author of 'Amy Herbert.' 8th Edition. Fcp. 5s.

**Thoughts for the Holy Week**, for Young Persons. By the same Author. 3d Edition. Fcp. 8vo. 2s.

**Night Lessons from Scripture.** By the same Author. 2d Edition. 32mo. 3s.

**Self-examination before Confirmation.** By the same Author. 32mo. 1s. 6d.

**Readings for a Month Preparatory to Confirmation** from Writers of the Early and English Church. By the same. Fcp. 4s.

**Readings for Every Day in Lent**, compiled from the Writings of Bishop JEREMY TAYLOR. By the same. Fcp. 5s.

**Preparation for the Holy Communion;** the Devotions chiefly from the works of JEREMY TAYLOR. By the same. 32mo. 3s.

**Morning Clouds.** Second Edition. Fcp. 5s.

**Spring and Autumn.** By the same Author. Post 8vo. 6s.

**The Wife's Manual;** or, Prayers, Thoughts, and Songs on Several Occasions of a Matron's Life. By the Rev. W. CALVERT, M.A. Crown 8vo. 10s. 6d.

**Spiritual Songs for the Sundays** and Holidays throughout the Year. By J. S. B. MONSELL, LL.D. Vicar of Egham. Fourth Edition. Fcp. 4s. 6d.

**The Beatitudes:** Abasement before God: Sorrow for Sin; Meekness of Spirit; Desire for Holiness; Gentleness; Purity of Heart; the Peace-makers; Sufferings for Christ. By the same. 2d Edition, fcp. 3s. 6d.

**Hymnologia Christiana;** or, Psalms and Hymns selected and arranged in the order of the Christian Seasons. By B. H. KENNEDY, D.D. Prebendary of Lichfield. Crown 8vo. 7s. 6d.

**Lyra Domestica;** Christian Songs for Domestic Edification. Translated from the *Psaltery and Harp* of C. J. P. SPITTA, and from other sources, by RICHARD MASSIE. FIRST and SECOND SERIES, fcp. 4s. 6d. each.

**Lyra Sacra;** Hymns, Ancient and Modern, Odes, and Fragments of Sacred Poetry. Edited by the Rev. B. W. SAVILE, M.A. Fcp. 5s.

**Lyra Germanica**, translated from the German by Miss C. WINKWORTH. FIRST SERIES, Hymns for the Sundays and Chief Festivals; SECOND SERIES, the Christian Life. Fcp. 5s. each SERIES.

**Hymns from Lyra Germanica**, 18mo. 1s.

**Historical Notes to the 'Lyra Germanica:'** containing brief Memoirs of the Authors of the Hymns, and Notices of Remarkable Occasions on which some of them have been used; with Notices of other German Hymn Writers. By THEODORE KÜBLER. Fcp. 7s. 6d.

**Lyra Eucharistica;** Hymns and Verses on the Holy Communion, Ancient and Modern; with other Poems. Edited by the Rev. ORBY SHIPLEY, M.A. Second Edition. Fcp. 7s. 6d.

**Lyra Messianica;** Hymns and Verses on the Life of Christ, Ancient and Modern; with other Poems. By the same Editor. Fcp. 7s. 6d.

**Lyra Mystica;** Hymns and Verses on Sacred Subjects, Ancient and Modern. By the same Editor. Fcp. 7s. 6d.

**The Chorale Book for England;** a complete Hymn-Book in accordance with the Services and Festivals of the Church of England: the Hymns translated by Miss C. WINKWORTH; the Tunes arranged by Prof. W. S. BENNETT and OTTO GOLDSCHMIDT. Fcp. 4to. 12s. 6d.

**Congregational Edition.** Fcp. 2s.

**The Catholic Doctrine of the Atonement;** an Historical Inquiry into its Development in the Church: with an Introduction on the Principle of Theological Developments. By H. N. OXENHAM, M.A. formerly Scholar of Balliol College, Oxford. 8vo. 8s. 6d.

**From Sunday to Sunday;** an attempt to consider familiarly the Weekday Life and Labours of a Country Clergyman. By R. GEE, M.A. Vicar of Abbott's Langley and Rural Dean. Fcp. 5s.

**First Sundays at Church;** or, Familiar Conversations on the Morning and Evening Services of the Church of England. By J. E. RIDDLE, M.A. Fcp. 2s. 6d.

**The Judgment of Conscience**, and other Sermons. By RICHARD WHATELY, D.D. late Archbishop of Dublin. Crown 8vo. 4s. 6d.

**Paley's Moral Philosophy**, with Annotations. By RICHARD WHATELY, D.D. late Archbishop of Dublin. 8vo. 7s.

## Travels, Voyages, &c.

**Outline Sketches of the High Alps of Dauphiné.** By T. G. BONNEY, M.A. F.G.S. M.A.C. Fellow of St. John's Coll. Camb. With 13 Plates and a Coloured Map. Post 4to. 16s.

**Ice Caves of France and Switzerland;** a narrative of Subterranean Exploration. By the Rev. G. F. BROWNE, M.A. Fellow and Assistant-Tutor of St. Catherine's Coll. Cambridge, M.A.C. With 11 Woodcuts. Square crown 8vo. 12s. 6d.

**Village Life in Switzerland.** By SOPHIA D. DELMARD. Post 8vo. 9s. 6d.

**How we Spent the Summer;** or, a Voyage en Zigzag in Switzerland and Tyrol with some Members of the ALPINE CLUB. From the Sketch-Book of one of the Party. In oblong 4to. with about 300 Illustrations, 10s. 6d.

**Map of the Chain of Mont Blanc,** from an actual Survey in 1863—1864. By A. ADAMS-REILLY, F.R.G.S. M.A.C. Published under the Authority of the Alpine Club. In Chromolithography on extra stout drawing-paper 28in. × 17in. price 10s. or mounted on canvas in a folding case, 12s. 6d.

**The Hunting Grounds of the Old World;** FIRST SERIES, *Asia*. By H. A. L. the Old Shekarry. Third Edition, with 7 Illustrations. 8vo. 18s.

**Camp and Cantonment;** a Journal of Life in India in 1857—1859, with some Account of the Way thither. By Mrs. LEOPOLD PAGET. To which is added a Short Narrative of the Pursuit of the Rebels in Central India by Major PAGET, R.H.A. Post 8vo. 10s. 6d.

**Explorations in South-west Africa,** from Walvisch Bay to Lake Ngami and the Victoria Falls. By THOMAS BAINES, F.R.G.S. 8vo. with Maps and Illustrations, 21s.

**South American Sketches;** or, a Visit to Rio Janeiro, the Organ Mountains, La Plata, and the Paraná. By THOMAS W. HINCHLIFF, M.A. F.R.G.S. Post 8vo. with Illustrations, 12s. 6d.

**Vancouver Island and British Columbia;** their History, Resources, and Prospects. By MATTHEW MACFIE, F.R.G.S. With Maps and Illustrations. 8vo. 18s.

**History of Discovery in our Australasian Colonies,** Australia, Tasmania, and New Zealand, from the Earliest Date to the Present Day. By WILLIAM HOWITT. With 3 Maps of the Recent Explorations from Official Sources. 2 vols. 8vo. 28s.

**The Capital of the Tycoon;** a Narrative of a 3 Years' Residence in Japan. By Sir RUTHERFORD ALCOCK, K.C.B. 2 vols. 8vo. with numerous Illustrations, 42s.

**Last Winter in Rome.** By C. R. WELD. With Portrait and Engravings on Wood. Post 8vo. 14s.

**Autumn Rambles in North Africa.** By JOHN ORMSBY, of the Middle Temple. With 16 Illustrations. Post 8vo. 8s. 6d.

**The Dolomite Mountains.** Excursions through Tyrol, Carinthia, Carniola, and Friuli in 1861, 1862, and 1863. By J. GILBERT and G. C. CHURCHILL, F.R.G.S. With numerous Illustrations. Square crown 8vo. 21s.

**A Summer Tour in the Grisons** and Italian Valleys of the Bernina. By Mrs. HENRY FRESHFIELD. With 2 Coloured Maps and 4 Views. Post 8vo. 10s. 6d.

**Alpine Byways;** or, Light Leaves gathered in 1859 and 1860. By the same Authoress. Post 8vo. with Illustrations, 10s. 6d.

**A Lady's Tour Round Monte Rosa;** including Visits to the Italian Valleys. With Map and Illustrations. Post 8vo. 14s.

**Guide to the Pyrenees,** for the use of Mountaineers. By CHARLES PACKE. With Maps, &c. and Appendix. Fcp. 6s.

**The Alpine Guide.** By JOHN BALL, M.R.I.A. late President of the Alpine Club. Post 8vo. with Maps and other Illustrations.

**Guide to the Western Alps,** including Mont Blanc, Monte Rosa, Zermatt, &c. 7s. 6d.

**Guide to the Oberland and all Switzerland,** excepting the Neighbourhood of Monte Rosa and the Great St. Bernard; with Lombardy and the adjoining portion of Tyrol. 7s. 6d.

**Christopher Columbus;** his Life, Voyages, and Discoveries. Revised Edition, with 4 Woodcuts. 18mo. 2s. 6d.

**Captain James Cook;** his Life, Voyages, and Discoveries. Revised Edition, with numerous Woodcuts. 18mo. 2s. 6d.

**Narratives of Shipwrecks of the** Royal Navy between 1793 and 1857, compiled from Official Documents in the Admiralty by W. O. S. GILLY; with a Preface by W. S. GILLY, D.D. 3rd Edition, fcp. 5s.

**A Week at the Land's End.** By J. T. BLIGHT; assisted by E. H. RODD, R. Q. COUCH, and J. RALFS. With Map and 96 Woodcuts. Fcp. 6s. 6d.

**Visits to Remarkable Places:** Old Halls, Battle-Fields, and Scenes illustrative of Striking Passages in English History and Poetry. By WILLIAM HOWITT. 2 vols. square crown 8vo. with Wood Engravings, 25s.

**The Rural Life of England.** By the same Author. With Woodcuts by Bewick and Williams. Medium 8vo. 12s. 6d.

---

## Works of Fiction.

**Late Laurels:** a Tale. By the Author of 'Wheat and Tares.' 2 vols. post 8vo. 15s.

**A First Friendship.** [Reprinted from *Fraser's Magazine.*] Crown 8vo. 7s. 6d.

**Atherstone Priory.** By L. N. COMYN. 2 vols. post 8vo. 21s.

**Ellice:** a Tale. By the same. Post 8vo. 9s. 6d.

**Stories and Tales by the Author** of 'Amy Herbert,' uniform Edition, each Tale or Story complete in a single volume.

AMY HERBERT, 2s. 6d.
GERTRUDE, 2s. 6d.
EARL'S DAUGHTER, 2s. 6d.
EXPERIENCE OF LIFE, 2s. 6d.
CLEVE HALL, 3s. 6d.
IVORS, 3s. 6d.
KATHARINE ASHTON, 3s. 6d.
MARGARET PERCIVAL, 5s.
LANETON PARSONAGE, 4s. 6d.
URSULA, 4s. 6d.

**A Glimpse of the World.** By the Author of 'Amy Herbert.' Fcp. 7s. 6d.

**Essays on Fiction,** reprinted chiefly from Reviews, with Additions. By NASSAU W. SENIOR. Post 8vo. 10s. 6d.

**Elihu Jan's Story;** or, the Private Life of an Eastern Queen. By WILLIAM KNIGHTON, LL.D. Assistant-Commissioner in Oudh. Post 8vo. 7s. 6d.

**The Six Sisters of the Valleys:** an Historical Romance. By W. BRAMLEY-MOORE, M.A. Incumbent of Gerrard's Cross, Bucks. Third Edition, with 14 Illustrations. Crown 8vo. 5s.

**The Gladiators:** a Tale of Rome and Judæa. By G. J. WHYTE MELVILLE. Crown 8vo. 5s.

**Digby Grand,** an Autobiography. By the same Author. 1 vol. 5s.

**Kate Coventry,** an Autobiography. By the same. 1 vol. 5s.

**General Bounce,** or the Lady and the Locusts. By the same. 1 vol. 5s.

**Holmby House,** a Tale of Old Northamptonshire. 1 vol. 5s.

**Good for Nothing,** or All Down Hill. By the same. 1 vol. 6s.

**The Queen's Maries,** a Romance of Holyrood. 1 vol. 6s.

**The Interpreter,** a Tale of the War. By the same. 1 vol. 5s.

**Tales from Greek Mythology.** By GEORGE W. COX, M.A. late Scholar of Trin. Coll. Oxon. Second Edition. Square 16mo. 3s. 6d.

**Tales of the Gods and Heroes.** By the same Author. Second Edition. Fcp. 5s.

**Tales of Thebes and Argos.** By the same Author. Fcp. 4s. 6d.

**The Warden:** a Novel. By ANTHONY TROLLOPE. Crown 8vo. 3s. 6d.

**Barchester Towers:** a Sequel to 'The Warden.' By the same Author. Crown 8vo. 5s.

## Poetry and the Drama.

**Select Works of the British Poets;** with Biographical and Critical Prefaces by Dr. AIKIN: with Supplement, of more recent Selections, by LUCY AIKIN. Medium 8vo. 18s.

**Goethe's Second Faust.** Translated by JOHN ANSTER, LL.D. M.R.I.A. Regius Professor of Civil Law in the University of Dublin. Post 8vo. 15s.

**Tasso's Jerusalem Delivered,** translated into English Verse by Sir J. KINGSTON JAMES, Kt. M.A. 2 vols. fcp. with Facsimile, 14s.

**Poetical Works of John Edmund** Reade; with final Revision and Additions. 3 vols. fcp. 18s. or each vol. separately, 6s.

**Moore's Poetical Works,** Cheapest Editions complete in 1 vol. including the Autobiographical Prefaces and Author's last Notes, which are still copyright. Crown 8vo. ruby type, with Portrait, 7s. 6d. or People's Edition, in larger type, 12s. 6d.

**Moore's Poetical Works,** as above, Library Edition, medium 8vo. with Portrait and Vignette, 14s. or in 10 vols. fcp. 3s. 6d. each

**Tenniel's Edition of Moore's** *Lalla Rookh,* with 68 Wood Engravings from Original Drawings and other Illustrations. Fcp. 4to. 21s.

**Moore's Lalla Rookh.** 32mo. Plate, 1s. 16mo. Vignette, 2s. 6d.

**Maclise's Edition of Moore's Irish** *Melodies,* with 161 Steel Plates from Original Drawings. Super-royal 8vo. 31s. 6d.

**Moore's Irish Melodies,** 32mo. Portrait, 1s. 16mo. Vignette, 2s. 6d.

**Southey's Poetical Works,** with the Author's last Corrections and copyright Additions. Library Edition, in 1 vol. medium 8vo. with Portrait and Vignette, 14s. or in 10 vols. fcp. 3s. 6d. each.

**Lays of Ancient Rome;** with *Ivry* and the *Armada.* By the Right Hon. LORD MACAULAY. 16mo. 4s. 6d.

**Lord Macaulay's Lays of Ancient** Rome. With 90 Illustrations on Wood, Original and from the Antique, from Drawings by G. SCHARF. Fcp. 4to. 21s.

**Poems.** By JEAN INGELOW. Ninth Edition. Fcp. 8vo. 5s.

**Poetical Works of Letitia Elizabeth** Landon (L.E.L.) 2 vols. 16mo. 10s.

**Playtime with the Poets:** a Selection of the best English Poetry for the use of Children. By a LADY. Crown 8vo. 5s.

**Bowdler's Family Shakspeare,** cheaper Genuine Edition, complete in 1 vol. large type, with 36 Woodcut Illustrations, price 14s. or, with the same ILLUSTRATIONS, in 6 pocket vols. 3s. 6d. each.

**Arundines Cami,** sive Musarum Cantabrigiensium Lusus Canori. Collegit atque edidit H. DRURY. M.A. Editio Sexta, curavit H. J. HODGSON. M.A. Crown 8vo. 7s. 6d.

## Rural Sports, &c.

**Encyclopædia of Rural Sports;** a Complete Account, Historical, Practical, and Descriptive, of Hunting, Shooting, Fishing, Racing, &c. By D. P. BLAINE. With above 600 Woodcuts (20 from Designs by JOHN LEECH). 8vo. 42s.

**Notes on Rifle Shooting.** By Captain HEATON, Adjutant of the Third Manchester Rifle Volunteer Corps. Fcp. 2s. 6d.

**Col. Hawker's Instructions to** Young Sportsmen in all that relates to Guns and Shooting. Revised by the Author's SON. Square crown 8vo. with Illustrations, 18s.

**The Dead Shot,** or Sportsman's Complete Guide; a Treatise on the Use of the Gun, Dog-breaking, Pigeon-shooting, &c. By MARKSMAN. Fcp. 8vo. with Plates, 5s.

**The Fly-Fisher's Entomology.**
By ALFRED RONALDS. With coloured Representations of the Natural and Artificial Insect. 6th Edition; with 20 coloured Plates. 8vo. 14s.

**Hand-book of Angling:** Teaching Fly-fishing, Trolling, Bottom-fishing, Salmon-fishing; with the Natural History of River Fish, and the best modes of Catching them. By EPHEMERA. Fcp. Woodcuts, 5s.

**The Cricket Field;** or, the History and the Science of the Game of Cricket. By JAMES PYCROFT, B.A. Trin. Coll. Oxon. 4th Edition. Fcp. 5s.

**The Cricket Tutor;** a Treatise exclusively Practical. By the same. 18mo. 1s.

**Cricketana.** By the same Author. With 7 Portraits of Cricketers. Fcp. 5s.

**The Horse:** with a Treatise on Draught. By WILLIAM YOUATT. New Edition, revised and enlarged. 8vo. with numerous Woodcuts, 10s. 6d.

**The Dog.** By the same Author. 8vo. with numerous Woodcuts, 6s.

**The Horse's Foot, and how to keep it Sound.** By W. MILES, Esq. 9th Edition, with Illustrations. Imp. 8vo. 12s. 6d.

**A Plain Treatise on Horse-shoeing.** By the same Author. Post 8vo. with Illustrations, 2s. 6d.

**Stables and Stable Fittings.** By the same. Imp. 8vo. with 13 Plates, 15s.

**Remarks on Horses' Teeth,** addressed to Purchasers. By the same. Post 8vo. 1s. 6d.

**On Drill and Manœuvres of Cavalry,** combined with Horse Artillery. By Major-Gen. MICHAEL W. SMITH, C.B. Commanding the Poonah Division of the Bombay Army. 8vo. 12s. 6d.

**The Dog in Health and Disease.** By STONEHENGE. With 70 Wood Engravings. Square crown 8vo. 15s.

**The Greyhound in 1864.** By the same Author. With 24 Portraits of Greyhounds. Square crown 8vo. 21s.

**The Ox,** his Diseases and their Treatment; with an Essay on Parturition in the Cow. By J. R. DOBSON, M.R.C.V.S. Crown 8vo. with Illustrations, 7s. 6d.

---

## *Commerce, Navigation, and Mercantile Affairs.*

**The Law of Nations Considered** as Independent Political Communities. By TRAVERS TWISS, D.C.L. Regius Professor of Civil Law in the University of Oxford. 2 vols. 8vo. 30s. or separately, PART I. *Peace*, 12s. PART II. *War*, 18s.

**A Nautical Dictionary, defining** the Technical Language relative to the Building and Equipment of Sailing Vessels and Steamers, &c. By ARTHUR YOUNG. Second Edition; with Plates and 150 Woodcuts. 8vo. 18s.

**A Dictionary, Practical, Theoretical, and Historical, of Commerce and Commercial Navigation.** By J. R. M'CULLOCH. 8vo. with Maps and Plans, 50s.

**The Study of Steam and the Marine Engine,** for Young Sea Officers. By S. M. SAXBY, R.N. Post 8vo. with 87 Diagrams, 5s. 6d.

**A Manual for Naval Cadets.** By J. M'NEIL BOYD, late Captain R.N. Third Edition; with 240 Woodcuts, and 11 coloured Plates. Post 8vo. 12s. 6d.

---

## *Works of Utility and General Information.*

**Modern Cookery for Private Families,** reduced to a System of Easy Practice in a Series of carefully-tested Receipts. By ELIZA ACTON. Newly revised and enlarged; with 8 Plates, Figures, and 150 Woodcuts. Fcp. 7s. 6d.

**The Handbook of Dining;** or, Corpulency and Leanness scientifically considered. By BRILLAT-SAVARIN, Author of 'Physiologie du Goût.' Translated by L. F. SIMPSON. Revised Edition, with Additions. Fcp. 8s. 6d.

NEW WORKS PUBLISHED BY LONGMANS AND CO.     19

**On Food and its Digestion;** an Introduction to Dietetics. By W. BRINTON, M.D. Physician to St. Thomas's Hospital, &c. With 48 Woodcuts. Post 8vo. 12s.

**Wine, the Vine, and the Cellar.** By THOMAS G. SHAW. Second Edition, revised and enlarged, with Frontispiece and 31 Illustrations on Wood. 8vo. 16s.

**A Practical Treatise on Brewing;** with Formulæ for Public Brewers, and Instructions for Private Families. By W. BLACK. 8vo. 10s. 6d.

**Short Whist.** By MAJOR A. The Sixteenth Edition, revised, with an Essay on the Theory of the Modern Scientific Game by PROF. P. Fcp. 3s. 6d.

**Whist, What to Lead.** By CAM. Second Edition. 32mo. 1s.

**Hints on Etiquette and the** Usages of Society; with a Glance at Bad Habits. Revised, with Additions, by a LADY of RANK. Fcp. 2s. 6d.

**The Cabinet Lawyer;** a Popular Digest of the Laws of England, Civil and Criminal. 20th Edition, extended by the Author; including the Acts of the Sessions 1863 and 1864. Fcp. 10s. 6d.

**The Philosophy of Health;** or, an Exposition of the Physiological and Sanitary Conditions conducive to Human Longevity and Happiness. By SOUTHWOOD SMITH, M.D. Eleventh Edition, revised and enlarged; with 113 Woodcuts. 8vo. 15s.

**Hints to Mothers on the Management** of their Health during the Period of Pregnancy and in the Lying-in Room. By T. BULL, M.D. Fcp. 5s.

**The Maternal Management of Children** in Health and Disease. By the same Author. Fcp. 5s.

**Notes on Hospitals.** By FLORENCE NIGHTINGALE. Third Edition, enlarged; with 13 Plans. Post 4to. 18s.

**C. M. Willich's Popular Tables** for Ascertaining the Value of Lifehold, Leasehold, and Church Property, Renewal Fines, &c.; the Public Funds; Annual Average Price and Interest on Consols from 1731 to 1861; Chemical, Geographical, Astronomical, Trigonometrical Tables, &c. Post 8vo. 10s.

**Thomson's Tables of Interest,** at Three, Four, Four and a Half, and Five per Cent., from One Pound to Ten Thousand and from 1 to 365 Days. 12mo. 3s. 6d.

**Maunder's Treasury of Knowledge** and Library of Reference: comprising an English Dictionary and Grammar, Universal Gazetteer, Classical Dictionary, Chronology, Law Dictionary, Synopsis of the Peerage, useful Tables, &c. Fcp. 10s.

## General and School Atlases.

**An Atlas of History and Geography,** representing the Political State of the World at successive Epochs from the commencement of the Christian Era to the Present Time, in a Series of 16 coloured Maps. By J. S. BREWER, M.A. Third Edition, revised, &c. by E. C. BREWER, LL.D. Royal 8vo. 15s.

**Bishop Butler's Atlas of Modern** Geography, in a Series of 33 full-coloured Maps, accompanied by a complete Alphabetical Index. New Edition, corrected and enlarged. Royal 8vo. 10s. 6d.

**Bishop Butler's Atlas of Ancient** Geography, in a Series of 24 full-coloured Maps, accompanied by a complete Accentuated Index. New Edition, corrected and enlarged. Royal 8vo. 12s.

**School Atlas of Physical, Political,** and Commercial Geography, in 17 full-coloured Maps, accompanied by descriptive Letterpress. By E. HUGHES F.R.A.S. Royal 8vo. 10s. 6d.

**Middle-Class Atlas of General** Geography, in a Series of 29 full-coloured Maps, containing the most recent Territorial Changes and Discoveries. By WALTER M'LEOD, F.R.G.S. 4to. 5s.

**Physical Atlas of Great Britain** and Ireland; comprising 30 full-coloured Maps, with illustrative Letterpress, forming a concise Synopsis of British Physical Geography. By WALTER M'LEOD, F.R.G.S. Fcp. 4to. 7s. 6d.

## Periodical Publications.

**The Edinburgh Review, or Critical Journal,** published Quarterly in January, April, July, and October. 8vo. price 6s. each No.

**The Geological Magazine, or** Monthly Journal of Geology, edited by HENRY WOODWARD, F.G.S.; assisted by Prof. J. MORRIS, F.G.S. and R. ETHERIDGE, F.R.S.E. F.G.S. 8vo. price 1s. each No.

**Fraser's Magazine for Town and Country,** published on the 1st of each Month. 8vo. price 2s. 6d. each No.

**The Alpine Journal:** a Record of Mountain Adventure and Scientific Observation. By Members of the Alpine Club. Edited by H. B. GEORGE, M.A. Published Quarterly, May 31, Aug. 31, Nov. 30, Feb. 28. 8vo. price 1s. 6d. each No.

---

## Knowledge for the Young.

**The Stepping Stone to Knowledge:** Containing upwards of Seven Hundred Questions and Answers on Miscellaneous Subjects, adapted to the capacity of Infant Minds. By a MOTHER. New Edition, enlarged and improved. 18mo. price 1s.

**The Stepping Stone to Geography:** Containing several Hundred Questions and Answers on Geographical Subjects. 18mo. 1s.

**The Stepping Stone to English History:** Containing several Hundred Questions and Answers on the History of England. 1s.

**The Stepping Stone to Bible Knowledge:** Containing several Hundred Questions and Answers on the Old and New Testaments. 18mo. 1s.

**The Stepping Stone to Biography:** Containing several Hundred Questions and Answers on the Lives of Eminent Men and Women. 18mo. 1s.

**Second Series of the Stepping Stone to Knowledge:** containing upwards of Eight Hundred Questions and Answers on Miscellaneous Subjects not contained in the FIRST SERIES. 18mo. 1s.

**The Stepping Stone to French Pronunciation and Conversation:** Containing several Hundred Questions and Answers. By Mr. P. SADLER. 18mo. 1s.

**The Stepping Stone to English Grammar:** containing several Hundred Questions and Answers on English Grammar. By Mr. P. SADLER. 18mo. 1s.

**The Stepping Stone to Natural History:** VERTEBRATE OR BACKBONED ANIMALS. PART I. *Mammalia;* PART II. *Birds, Reptiles, Fishes.* 18mo. 1s. each Part.

**The Instructor;** or, Progressive Lessons in General Knowledge. Originally published under the Direction of the Committee of General Literature and Education of the Society for Promoting Christian Knowledge. 7 vols. 18mo. freely illustrated with Woodcuts and Maps, price 14s.

I. **Exercises, Tales, and Conversations** on Familiar Subjects; with Easy Lessons from History. Revised and improved Edition. Price 2s.

II. **Lessons on Dwelling-Houses and** the Materials used in Building Them; on Articles of Furniture; and on Food and Clothing. Revised and improved Edition. Price 2s.

III. **Lessons on the Universe;** on the Three Kingdoms of Nature, Animal, Vegetable, and Mineral; on the Structure, Senses, and Habits of Man; and on the Preservation of Health. Revised and improved Edition. 2s.

IV. **Lessons on the Calendar and Almanack;** on the Twelve Months of the Year; and on the appearances of Nature in the Four Seasons, Spring, Summer, Autumn, and Winter. Revised and improved Edition. Price 2s.

V. **Descriptive Geography with Popular Statistics** of the various Countries and Divisions of the Globe, their People and Productions. Revised and improved Edition. With 6 Maps. 2s.

VI. **Elements of Ancient History,** from the Formation of the First Great Monarchies to the Fall of the Roman Empire. Revised and improved Edition. Price 2s.

VII. **Elements of [Mediæval and] Modern History,** from A.D. 406 to A.D. 1862: with brief Notices of European Colonies. Revised and improved Edition. Price 2s.

# INDEX.

ABBOTT on Sight and Touch .............. 6
ACTON's Modern Cookery ............... 18
AIKIN's Select British Poets .............. 17
——— Memoirs and Remains............ 3
ALCOCK's Residence in Japan.............. 15
ALLIES on Formation of Christianity ...... 13
Alpine Guide (The) ...................... 15
——— Journal (The) .................... 20
APJOHN's Manual of the Metalloids........ 8
ARAGO's Biographies of Scientific Men .... 4
——— Popular Astronomy .............. 7
——— Meteorological Essays'............ 7
ARNOLD's Manual of English Literature.... 5
ARNOTT's Elements of Physics ............ 8
Arundines Cami ......................... 17
Atherstone Priory ....................... 16
ATKINSON's Papinian .................... 4
Autumn Holidays of a Country Parson .... 6
AYRE's Treasury of Bible Knowledge ...... 13

BABBAGE's Life of a Philosopher .......... 3
BACON's Essays, by WHATELY ............ 4
——— Life and Letters, by SPEDDING.... 3
——— Works, by ELLIS, SPEDDING, and HEATH.................................. 4
BAIN on the Emotions and Will............ 6
——— on the Senses and Intellect ........ 6
——— on the Study of Character .......... 6
BAINES's Explorations in S.W. Africa .... 15
BALL's Guide to the Central Alps.......... 15
———Guide to the Western Alps ........ 15
BAYLDON's Rents and Tillages ............ 12
BLACK's Treatise on Brewing.............. 19
BLACKLEY and FRIEDLANDER's German and English Dictionary.................. 5
BLAINE's Rural Sports.................... 17
BLIGHT's Week at the Land's End ........ 16
BONNEY's Alps of Dauphiné .............. 15
BOURNE's Catechism of the Steam Engine.. 12
——— Handbook of Steam Engine .... 12
——— Treatise on the Steam Engine.... 11
BOWDLER's Family SHAKSPEARE.......... 17
BOYD's Manual for Naval Cadets .......... 18
BRAMLEY-MOORE's Six Sisters of the Valleys 16
BRANDE's Dictionary of Science, Literature, and Art .................................. 9
BRAY's (C.) Education of the Feelings...... 7
——— Philosophy of Necessity........ 7
——— (Mrs.) British Empire ............ 7
BREWER's Atlas of History and Geography 19
BRINTON on Food and Digestion .......... 19
BRISTOW's Glossary of Mineralogy ........ 8
BRODIE's (Sir C. B.) Psychological Inquiries 7
——— ——— Works................ 10
——— ——— Autobiography........ 10
BROWNE's Ice Caves of France and Switzerland .................................... 15

BROWNE's Exposition 39 Articles .......... 12
——— Pentateuch ..................... 12
BUCKLE's History of Civilization .......... 2
BULL's Hints to Mothers................... 19
——— Maternal Management of Children.. 19
BUNSEN's Analecta Ante-Nicæna .......... 13
——— Ancient Egypt.................... 2
——— Hippolytus and his Age ........ 13
——— Philosophy of Universal History 13
BUNSEN on Apocrypha.................... 13
BUNYAN's Pilgrim's Progress, illustrated by BENNETT ................................ 11
BURKE's Vicissitudes of Families .......... 4
BURTON's Christian Church .............. 3
BUTLER's Atlas of Ancient Geography .... 19
——— Modern Geography............. 19

Cabinet Lawyer............................ 19
CALVERT's Wife's Manual ................ 14
Campaigner at Home...................... 6
CATS and FARLIE's Moral Emblems ........ 11
Chorale Book for England ................ 14
COLENSO (Bishop) on Pentateuch and Book of Joshua................................ 13
COLUMBUS's Voyages...................... 16
Commonplace Philosopher in Town and Country .................................. 6
CONINGTON's Handbook of Chemical Analysis ..................................... 9
CONTANSEAU's Pocket French and English Dictionary ................................ 5
——— Practical ditto ............ 5
CONYBEARE and HOWSON's Life and Epistles of St. Paul .............................. 12
COOK's Voyages .......................... 16
COPLAND's Dictionary of Practical Medicine 10
——— Abridgment of ditto .............. 10
Cox's Tales of the Great Persian War ...... 2
——— Tales from Greek Mythology........ 16
——— Tales of the Gods and Heroes........ 16
——— Tales of Thebes and Argos ........ 16
CRESY's Encyclopædia of Civil Engineering 11
Critical Essays of a Country Parson........ 6
CROWE's History of France................ 2

D'AUBIGNÉ's History of the Reformation in the time of CALVIN ...................... 2
Dead Shot (The), by MARKSMAN .......... 17
DE LA RIVE's Treatise on Electricity ...... 8
DELMARD's Village Life in Switzerland.... 15
DE LA PRYME's Life of Christ ............ 13
DE TOCQUEVILLE's Democracy in America 2
Diaries of a Lady of Quality................ 3
DOBSON on the Ox ...................... 18
DOVE's Law of Storms .................... 7
DOYLE's Chronicle of England ............ 2

Edinburgh Review (The) .................. 20
Ellice, a Tale............................. 16
ELLICOTT's Broad and Narrow Way........ 13
———— —— Commentary on Ephesians .... 13
———— ———— Destiny of the Creature........ 13
———— ———— Lectures on Life of Christ ..... 13
———— ———— Commentary on Galatians .... 13
———— ———— ———— Pastoral Epist. 13
———— ———— ———— Philippians,&c. 13
———— ———— ———— Thessalonians 13
Essays and Reviews ........................ 13
———— on Religion and Literature, edited by
  MANNING ................................ 13
———— written in the Intervals of Business 6

FAIRBAIRN's Application of Cast and
  Wrought Iron to Building.............. 11
———— ———— Information for Engineers .. 11
———— ———— Treatise on Mills & Millwork 11
FFOULKES's Christendom's Divisions ...... 13
First Friendship .......................... 16
FITZ ROY's Weather Book ................. 7
FOWLER's Collieries and Colliers .......... 12
Fraser's Magazine ......................... 20
FRESHFIELD's Alpine Byways ............... 15
———— ———— Tour in the Grisons ........ 15
Friends in Council ........................ 6
FROUDE's History of England.............. 1

GARRATT's Marvels and Mysteries of Instinct 8
GEE's Sunday to Sunday ................... 14
Geological Magazine.................... 8, 20
GILBERT and CHURCHILL's Dolomite Mountains ...................................... 15
GILLY's Shipwrecks of the Navy ........... 16
GOETHE's Second Faust, by Anster........ 17
GOODEVE's Elements of Mechanism........ 11
GORLE's Questions on BROWNE's Exposition
  of the 39 Articles ....................... 12
Graver Thoughts of a Country Parson ...... 6
GRAY's Anatomy........................... 10
GREENE's Corals and Sea Jellies ........... 8
———— Sponges and Animalculae ...... 8
GROVE on Correlation of Physical Forces .. 8
GWILT's Encyclopædia of Architecture .... 11

Handbook of Angling, by EPHEMERA...... 18
HARE on Election of Representatives ...... 5
HARTWIG's Sea and its Living Wonders.... 8
———— ———— Tropical World ............. 8
HAWKER's Instructions to Young Sportsmen ...................................... 17
HEATON's Notes on Rifle Shooting ........ 17
HELPS's Spanish Conquest in America .... 2
HERSCHEL's Essays from the Edinburgh and
  Quarterly Reviews ...................... 9
———— ———— Outlines of Astronomy........ 7
HEWITT on the Diseases of Women ........ 9
HINCHLIFF's South American Sketches.... 15
Hints on Etiquette ........................ 19
HODGSON's Time and Space................ 7
HOLLAND's Chapters on Mental Physiology 6
———— ———— Essays on Scientific Subjects .. 9
———— ———— Medical Notes and Reflections 10
HOLMES's System of Surgery............... 10
HOOKER and WALKER-ARNOTT's British
  Flora.................................... 9
HORNE's Introduction to the Scriptures.... 13

HORNE's Compendium of the Scriptures .. 13
HOSKYNS's Talpa ......................... 12
How we Spent the Summer................. 15
HOWITT's Australian Discovery .......... 15
———— ———— History of the Supernatural .... 6
———— ———— Rural Life of England .......... 16
———— ———— Visits to Remarkable Places .... 16
HOWSON's Hulsean Lectures on St. Paul..... 12
HUGHES's (E.) Atlas of Physical, Political,
  and Commercial Geography.............. 19
———— (W.) Geography of British History ..................................... 7
———— ———— Manual of Geography ...... 7
HULLAH's History of Modern Music ...... 3
———— ———— Transition Musical Lectures ...... 3
HUMPHREYS' Sentiments of Shakspeare.... 11
Hunting Grounds of the Old World ........ 15
Hymns from Lyra Germanica.............. 14

INGELOW's Poems ......................... 17
Instructor (The) .......................... 20

JAMESON's Legends of the Saints and Martyrs ...................................... 11
———— ———— Legends of the Madonna .. 11
———— ———— Legends of the Monastic Orders 11
JAMESON and EASTLAKE's History of Our
  Lord .................................... 11
JOHNS's Home Walks and Holiday Rambles 9
JOHNSON's Patentee's Manual ............. 11
———— ———— Practical Draughtsman ........ 11
JOHNSTON's Gazetteer, or Geographical Dictionary.................................... 7
JONES's Christianity and Common Sense .. 7

KALISCH's Commentary on the Old Testament........................................ 5
———— ———— Hebrew Grammar............. 5
KENNEDY's Hymnologia Christiana ...... 14
KESTEVEN's Domestic Medicine .......... 10
KIRBY and SPENCE's Entomology ........ 9
KNIGHTON's Story of Elihu Jan .......... 16
KIDDER's Notes to Lyra Germanica....... 14
KUENEN on Pentateuch and Joshua........ 13

Lady's Tour round Monte Rosa............. 15
LANDON's (L. E. L.) Poetical Works........ 17
Late Laurels .............................. 16
LATHAM's English Dictionary ............. 5
LECKY's History of Rationalism .......... 2
Leisure Hours in Town .................... 6
LEWES's Biographical History of Philosophy 2
LEWIS on the Astronomy of the Ancients .. 4
———— on the Credibility of Early Roman
  History ................................. 4
———— ———— Dialogue on Government........... 4
———— ———— on Egyptological Method............ 4
———— ———— Essays on Administrations ........ 4
———— ———— Fables of BABRIUS................. 4
———— ———— on Foreign Jurisdiction ........... 4
———— ———— on Irish Disturbances ............ 4
———— ———— on Observation and Reasoning in
  Politics.................................. 4
———— ———— on Political Terms ................. 4
———— ———— on the Romance Languages ...... 4
LIDDELL and SCOTT's Greek-English Lexicon 5
———— ———— ———— Abridged ditto ...... 5
LINDLEY and MOORE's Treasury of Botany. 9

| | |
|---|---|
| Longman's Lectures on the History of England | 1 |
| Loudon's Encyclopædia of Agriculture | 12 |
| ——————— Cottage, Farm, and Villa Architecture | 12 |
| ——————— Gardening | 12 |
| ——————— Plants | 9 |
| ——————— Trees and Shrubs | 9 |
| Lowndes's Engineer's Handbook | 11 |
| Lyra Domestica | 14 |
| —— Eucharistica | 14 |
| —— Germanica | 11, 14 |
| —— Messianica | 14 |
| —— Mystica | 14 |
| —— Sacra | 14 |
| | |
| Macaulay's (Lord) Essays | 2 |
| ——————— History of England | 1 |
| ——————— Lays of Ancient Rome | 17 |
| ——————— Miscellaneous Writings | 6 |
| ——————— Speeches | 5 |
| ——————— Speeches on Parliamentary Reform | 5 |
| Macdougall's Theory of War | 12 |
| Marshman's Life of Havelock | 3 |
| McLeod's Middle-Class Atlas of General Geography | 19 |
| ——————— Physical Atlas of Great Britain and Ireland | 19 |
| McCulloch's Dictionary of Commerce | 18 |
| ——————— Geographical Dictionary | 7 |
| Macfie's Vancouver Island | 15 |
| Maguire's Life of Father Mathew | 3 |
| ——————— Rome and its Rulers | 3 |
| Maling's Indoor Gardener | 9 |
| Massey's History of England | 1 |
| Massingberd's History of the Reformation | 3 |
| Maunder's Biographical Treasury | 4 |
| ——————— Geographical Treasury | 7 |
| ——————— Historical Treasury | 2 |
| ——————— Scientific and Literary Treasury | 9 |
| ——————— Treasury of Knowledge | 19 |
| ——————— Treasury of Natural History | 9 |
| Maury's Physical Geography | 7 |
| May's Constitutional History of England | 1 |
| Melville's Digby Grand | 16 |
| ——————— General Bounce | 16 |
| ——————— Gladiators | 16 |
| ——————— Good for Nothing | 16 |
| ——————— Holmby House | 16 |
| ——————— Interpreter | 16 |
| ——————— Kate Coventry | 16 |
| ——————— Queen's Maries | 16 |
| Mendelssohn's Letters | 3 |
| Menzies' Windsor Great Park | 12 |
| ——————— on Sewage | 12 |
| Merivale's (H.) Colonisation and Colonies | 7 |
| ——————— Historical Studies | 1 |
| ——————— (C.) Fall of the Roman Republic | 2 |
| ——————— Romans under the Empire | 2 |
| ——————— on Conversion of Roman Empire | 2 |
| ——————— on Horse's Foot | 18 |
| ——————— on Horse Shoeing | 18 |
| ——————— on Horses' Teeth | 18 |
| ——————— on Stables | 18 |
| Mill on Liberty | 4 |
| ——— on Representative Government | 4 |
| ——— on Utilitarianism | 4 |

| | |
|---|---|
| Mill's Dissertations and Discussions | 4 |
| ——— Political Economy | 4 |
| ——— System of Logic | 4 |
| ——— Hamilton's Philosophy | 4 |
| Miller's Elements of Chemistry | 9 |
| Monsell's Spiritual Songs | 14 |
| ——— Beatitudes | 14 |
| Montagu's Experiments in Church and State | 13 |
| Montgomery on the Signs and Symptoms of Pregnancy | 9 |
| Moore's Irish Melodies | 17 |
| ——— Lalla Rookh | 17 |
| ——— Memoirs, Journal, and Correspondence | 3 |
| ——— Poetical Works | 17 |
| Morell's Elements of Psychology | 6 |
| ——— Mental Philosophy | 6 |
| Morning Clouds | 14 |
| Morton's Prince Consort's Farms | 12 |
| Mosheim's Ecclesiastical History | 13 |
| Müller's (Max) Lectures on the Science of Language | 5 |
| ——— (K. O.) Literature of Ancient Greece | 2 |
| Murchison on Continued Fevers | 10 |
| Mure's Language and Literature of Greece | 2 |
| | |
| New Testament illustrated with Wood Engravings from the Old Masters | 10 |
| Newman's History of his Religious Opinions | 3 |
| Nightingale's Notes on Hospitals | 19 |
| | |
| Odling's Course of Practical Chemistry | 9 |
| ——— Manual of Chemistry | 9 |
| Ormsby's Rambles in Algeria and Tunis | 15 |
| Owen's Comparative Anatomy and Physiology of Vertebrate Animals | 6 |
| Oxenham on Atonement | 14 |
| | |
| Packe's Guide to the Pyrenees | 15 |
| Paget's Lectures on Surgical Pathology | 10 |
| ——— Camp and Cantonment | 15 |
| Pereira's Elements of Materia Medica | 10 |
| ——— Manual of Materia Medica | 10 |
| Perkins's Tuscan Sculpture | 11 |
| Phillips's Guide to Geology | 8 |
| ——— Introduction to Mineralogy | 8 |
| Piesse's Art of Perfumery | 12 |
| ——— Chemical, Natural, and Physical Magic | 12 |
| ——— Laboratory of Chemical Wonders | 12 |
| Playtime with the Poets | 17 |
| Practical Mechanic's Journal | 11 |
| Prescott's Scripture Difficulties | 13 |
| Proctor's Saturn | 7 |
| Pycroft's Course of English Reading | 5 |
| ——— Cricket Field | 18 |
| ——— Cricket Tutor | 18 |
| ——— Cricketana | 18 |
| | |
| Reade's Poetical Works | 17 |
| Recreations of a Country Parson, Second Series | 6 |
| Reilly's Map of Mont Blanc | 15 |
| Riddle's Diamond Latin-English Dictionary | 5 |
| ——— First Sundays at Church | 14 |
| Rivers's Rose Amateur's Guide | 9 |

# NEW WORKS published by LONGMANS and CO.

ROGERS's Correspondence of Greyson ...... 6
———— Eclipse of Faith ................. 6
———— Defence of ditto ............... 6
———— Essays from the *Edinburgh Review* 6
———— Fulleriana ..................... 6
ROGET's Thesaurus of English Words and Phrases .................................. 5
RONALDS's Fly-Fisher's Entomology ...... 18
ROWTON's Debater ....................... 5
RUSSELL on Government and Constitution . 1

SAXBY's Study of Steam ................. 18
———— Weather System ............... 7
SCOTT's Handbook of Volumetric Analysis 9
SCROPE on Volcanos ..................... 8
SENIOR's Biographical Sketches ......... 4
———— Historical and Philosophical Essays ................................ 2
———— Essays on Fiction .............. 16
SEWELL's Amy Herbert .................. 16
———— Ancient History ................ 2
———— Cleve Hall ..................... 16
———— Earl's Daughter ................ 16
———— Experience of Life ............. 16
———— Gertrude ....................... 16
———— Glimpse of the World .......... 16
———— History of the Early Church .... 3
———— Ivors .......................... 16
———— Katharine Ashton ............... 16
———— Laneton Parsonage .............. 16
———— Margaret Percival .............. 16
———— Night Lessons from Scripture ... 14
———— Passing Thoughts on Religion ... 14
———— Preparation for Communion ..... 14
———— Readings for Confirmation ..... 14
———— Readings for Lent .............. 14
———— Self-Examination before Confirmation ............................ 14
———— Stories and Tales .............. 16
———— Thoughts for the Holy Week .... 14
———— Ursula ......................... 16
SHAW's Work on Wine ................... 19
SHEDDEN's Elements of Logic ............ 5
Short Whist ........................... 19
SHORT's Church History ................. 3
SIEVEKING's (AMELIA) Life, by WINKWORTH ................................ 3
SIMPSON's Handbook of Dining .......... 18
SMITH's (SOUTHWOOD) Philosophy of Health 19
———— (J.) Voyage and Shipwreck of St. Paul .................................. 13
———— (G.) Wesleyan Methodism ........ 3
———— (SYDNEY) Memoir and Letters ... 4
———— ———— Miscellaneous Works .. —
———— ———— Sketches of Moral Philosophy ................................ 6
———— ———— Wit and Wisdom ......... 6
SMITH on Cavalry Drill and Manœuvres ... 18
SOUTHEY's (Doctor) ..................... 5
———— ———— Poetical Works .......... 17
SPOHR's Autobiography ................... 3
Spring and Autumn ..................... 14
STANLEY's History of British Birds ...... 8
STEBBING's Analysis of MILL's Logic ..... 5
STEPHENSON's (R.) Life by JEAFFRESON and POLE ............................ 3
STEPHEN's Essays in Ecclesiastical Biography .............................. 4

STEPHEN's Lectures on the History of France ................................ 2
Stepping Stone to Knowledge, &c ........ 20
STIRLING's Secret of Hegel ............. 6
STONEHENGE on the Dog ................. 18
———— on the Greyhound ............ 18

TASSO's Jerusalem, by JAMES ............ 17
TAYLOR's (Jeremy) Works, edited by EDEN 14
TENNENT's Ceylon ....................... 8
———— Natural History of Ceylon .... 8
THIRLWALL's History of Greece ......... 2
THOMSON's (Archbishop) Laws of Thought 4
———— (J.) Tables of Interest ........ 19
———— Conspectus, by BIRKETT ....... 10
TODD's Cyclopædia of Anatomy and Physiology .................................. 10
———— and BOWMAN's Anatomy and Physiology of Man ......................... 10
TROLLOPE's Barchester Towers .......... 16
———— Warden ....................... 16
TWISS's Law of Nations ................. 18
TYNDALL's Lectures on Heat ............. 8

URE's Dictionary of Arts, Manufactures, and Mines .................................. 11

VAN DER HOEVEN's Handbook of Zoology 8
VAUGHAN's (R.) Revolutions in English History .................................. 1
———— (R. A.) Hours with the Mystics 7
VILLARI's Savonarola ................... 3

WATSON's Principles and Practice of Physic 10
WATTS's Dictionary of Chemistry ........ 9
WEBB's Celestial Objects for Common Telescopes ................................ 7
WEBSTER & WILKINSON's Greek Testament 13
WELD's Last Winter in Rome ............ 15
WELLINGTON's Life, by BRIALMONT and GLEIG .................................. 3
———— ———— by GLEIG ............ 3
WEST on the Diseases of Infancy and Childhood .................................. 9
WHATELY's English Synonymes .......... 4
———— Logic ......................... 4
———— Remains ....................... 4
———— Rhetoric ...................... 4
———— Sermons ....................... 14
———— Paley's Moral Philosophy .... 14
WHEWELL's History of the Inductive Sciences ................................ 2
Whist, what to lead, by CAM ........... 19
WHITE and RIDDLE's Latin-English Dictionary ................................ 5
WILBERFORCE (W.) Recollections of, by HARFORD .............................. 3
WILLIAMS's Superstitions of Witchcraft .. 6
WILLICH's Popular Tables ............... 19
WILSON's Bryologia Britannica ......... 9
WOOD's Homes without Hands ........... 8
WOODWARD's Historical and Chronological Encyclopædia ......................... 2

YONGE's English-Greek Lexicon ......... 5
———— Abridged ditto ............... 5
YOUNG's Nautical Dictionary ............ 18
YOUATT on the Dog ..................... 13
———— on the Horse ................. 13

www.ingramcontent.com/pod-product-compliance
Lightning Source LLC
Chambersburg PA
CBHW020130170426
43199CB00010B/709